simple ways to success

family

Silvana Franco

photography by Gus Filgate

This edition first published in 2003 by Quadrille Publishing Limited
Alhambra House 27-31 Charing Cross Road London WC2H OLS

Editorial director Jane O'Shea **Creative director** Helen Lewis
Managing editor Janet Illsley **Art direction** Vanessa Courtier
Editor Norma Macmillan **Designer** Sue Storey **Photographer** Gus Filgate
Food stylist Silvana Franco, **assisted by** Anna-Lisa Aldridge
Props stylist Jane Campsie **Production** Vincent Smith and Jane Rogers

Cataloguing in Publication Data: a catalogue record for this book is available from the British Library.

ISBN 1 84400 070 2
Printed in China

contents

introduction **6**

easy family cooking **8**

1   breakfasts **12**

2   everyday suppers **30**

3   weekends **70**

4   lunchboxes and snacks **102**

5   just for two **124**

6   family feasts **142**

7   puddings **166**

index **190**

NOTES

All spoon measures are level unless otherwise stated:
1 teaspoon = 5 ml spoon; 1 tablespoon = 15 ml spoon.

Use fresh herbs unless dried herbs are suggested.

Use sea salt and freshly ground black pepper unless otherwise stated.

Free-range eggs are recommended and large eggs should be used
except where a different size is specified.

Recipes which feature raw or lightly cooked eggs should be avoided by
anyone who is pregnant or in a vulnerable health group.

introduction

Meal times in my home have never followed a pattern. Sometimes I find myself alone with a hot sausage sandwich smothered in mustard, eyes glued to the television screen, other times the house is packed with my yelling nephews using breadsticks as swords and dropping dollops of cheese dip on my newly sanded floor. From one day to the next, family meal times vary, not just in the time of day but who's eating and how long you've got to prepare the meal.

The best piece of advice I can offer is be prepared and whatever happens (and it will go belly-up at times) don't worry about it. Because family meal times are about wholesome, hearty and delicious home-cooked dishes that aren't out to impress but to fill hungry bellies. Enjoy cooking the food and take pleasure from your family's enjoyment of what you give them. And don't worry if the pastry cracks or the cheesecake sinks – real, home-cooked food is charming and packed with personality, and you can be sure that it's going to taste fantastic.

Most of the recipes in this book are really easy and pretty quick too. In fact most of them, certainly in the 'everyday suppers' and 'just for two' chapters, go from shopping bag to table in just 30 minutes. All the recipes are easy-to-follow, packed with shortcuts and make good use of everyday ingredients, including some good quality convenience foods, such as ready-made pastry, curry paste and pizza dough mix. And for those occasions when you do feel like pushing the boat out a little and have a bit more time on your hands, then the 'weekends' chapter is packed with dishes that are stylish enough for entertaining yet still uncomplicated. There are no huge lists of ingredients or time-consuming techniques here, just scrumptious tarts and plenty of slow-cooked meat dishes.

Many of the recipes in this book belie my upbringing in a large Italian family where daily life focused round the hustle and bustle of the kitchen. Despite having plenty of other rooms in the house my siblings and I would jostle for elbow space on the work surface next to the bubbling pot of rosemary scented broth. Like most people, I learned to cook from watching my mum and helping with the simpler tasks. Her classic southern Italian cooking is now incredibly popular in this country and it's influence on me is evident throughout this book.

Alongside Mediterranean dishes, including mum's spaghetti with mussels (page 33), you'll also find my best English family dishes such as crusty-topped shepherds pie (page 163) and treacle tart, illustrated opposite (recipe, page 187). There's also lots of quick favourites that I turn to again and again like stir-fried steak chilli (page 54). Whenever I have great-tasting food in restaurants or cooked for me by friends, I try to recreate the dish myself at home – silky chicken noodle soup (page 77) and salt and pepper spare ribs (page 93) are two examples.

There's an old saying in Italy that 'food only tastes good and cakes only rise well if you cook with a happy heart'. I hope cooking and eating from this collection of my favourite recipes makes your heart as happy as it makes mine.

easy family cooking

Preparation is the key to hassle-free family cooking and the first step is to sort the storecupboard, fridge and freezer. Then assess your equipment, and decide if you need more tools to make your life easier. A little time spent in getting prepared will save you a lot of time later.

Taking stock

Begin by assessing what you've got in stock and then having a good clearout. In the storecupboard, get rid of anything that's out of date and ditch multiples of things you'll never use up, like spices and dried herbs. Be ruthless and throw out anything you know you're unlikely to use, however exciting or exotic. That can of guavas may sound wonderful, but is it going to be opened soon or will it linger in the back of the cupboard until it's past its best? If you really can't bear to part with some dried goods that you feel sure will come in handy, give them one week's stay of execution. After that get rid of them.

The same goes for the freezer. We're all guilty of letting the frost build up next to the ice trays. Now is the time for a clearout. If you must, give the best items one week's grace, but then unplug the freezer, defrost it fully and clean it. After this you can think about refilling it. The fridge is not usually in such a sorry state, simply because it's used more frequently. But most of us could still do with clearing out some of those neglected opened jars of sauces, pickles and pastes taking up space on the top shelf.

When you go shopping, think about what you'll need over the next few days. Decide what dishes you're going to cook and plan your shopping list around them. Also start restocking the foods you want to keep in store. If you have a well-stocked fridge and storecupboard, and a few standby dishes in the freezer, you'll always be able to feed your family without too much trouble.

The storecupboard

Keeping a good supply of essential foodstuffs will guarantee that you can rustle up a speedy supper, however basic. While it's true that many products now can be kept for a long time, it's a good idea to try to keep quantities at a realistic minimum in order to avoid wastage – an average-size bag, can, jar or bottle will do for most families. The only exception to this in my own pantry is canned tomatoes, which I buy by the truckload because I use them so often. If possible have a rack in a larder or cool cupboard for storing sturdy vegetables such as onions, potatoes and carrots that don't belong in the fridge. Take them out of any plastic packaging and arrange in the rack so air can circulate round them.

The following is a list of my suggestions for storecupboard standbys. There are sure to be some foods you wouldn't use and a few missing items that your family wouldn't be without – perhaps peanut butter.

Bottles and jars Sunflower oil, olive oil, extra virgin olive oil, toasted sesame oil, white wine vinegar, soy sauce, chilli sauce, Thai fish sauce, curry paste, mayonnaise, tomato ketchup, mustard, honey, wine.

Cans Plum tomatoes, tuna in spring water, anchovies in oil, baked beans, chick peas, cannellini beans, red kidney beans, coconut milk.

Dried goods Spaghetti or linguine, plus selection of pasta shapes (penne, fusilli etc), noodles, long-grain rice, risotto rice, red lentils, stock cubes, selection of dried herbs and spices, plain flour, baking powder, cornflour, sea salt, black peppercorns, caster sugar, muscovado sugar, sultanas, selection of nuts.

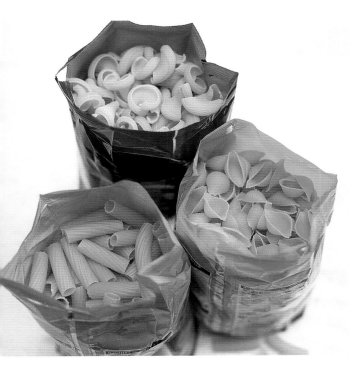

In the chill

Although the storecupboard needs the most careful planning, the fridge and freezer will need some reorganising too. Stock the fridge with your daily basics, plus any special ingredients you need for dishes you're planning to cook that week. You'll no doubt build up a collection of opened jars and bottles again, but routinely check them to be sure they are still eatable. Also carefully look through each shelf and drawer on a regular basis – there's nothing quite as unpleasant as coming across a waterlogged chunk of cucumber. Make sure all food is closely covered, particularly strong-smelling items whose odour could permeate other foods.

The freezer is your saviour when it comes to those bank holidays when you find the fridge is empty by Sunday night, or rainy days when you can't face a trip to the shops. Supermarket freezers are packed with really useful ingredients that you can keep for up to three months and almost everything else you can buy is labelled to show whether or not it's suitable for the freezer. My freezer is never without a packet of flatbreads, garden peas, broad beans, mince, frozen pastry, vanilla ice cream and plenty of ice.

However, without a bit of strict management the freezer will easily reach bursting point within weeks of clearing it out. I find the best solution to this is to divide the space in half, and to use one half for fantastically useful ingredients, such as frozen vegetables and pastry, and the other half for dishes I have cooked myself. Every once in a while, I make a concerted effort to eat every prepared meal in the freezer before freezing any more.

Equipment

Having cleared out and re-organised your stocks of food, you can then move on to assess your kitchen equipment and utensils. Apart from cutlery and crockery, you don't usually need multiples of things, and there is a fine line between useful gadgets that make cooking more efficient and other, not so handy items. These are the ones we all have tucked away at the back of the cupboard or drawer or hidden under the stairs gathering dust. Of course our individual lifestyles play a large part in whether or not these tools will ever be used, so you have to decide on this yourself.

I have an electric juicer that's so worn out I'm too ashamed to have it on the work top. So I keep it in a cupboard and lug it out each time I need it. Indeed, a good way of knowing whether or not to keep a piece of equipment is to position it on your work surface. If after a week it hasn't seen any action at all, then it's off to the charity shop with it. Before purchasing any large electrical items, such as a bread maker or a heavy-duty electric mixer that's marvellous for making cakes, think about it carefully. These appliances are expensive, take up a lot of room and are only worth having if you are going to use them often.

Here's my recommended batterie of basic equipment. The extras, such as juicers and blenders, are up to you. Remember, though, that many items in a basic kit are multi-functional – if you've got a good non-stick frying pan, why give up valuable cupboard space, and hard-earned cash, for a sandwich toaster?

Basic kit

A decent set of knives is a must for any cook. Buy good-quality knives that feel comfortable in your grip and make sure you keep them sharp – I recommend you get them professionally sharpened every couple of months. Before too long, even if you're pretty handy with a sharpening steel, your knives won't sharpen and will eventually need properly grinding.

You also need general equipment such as bowls, chopping boards, a colander, a grater and utensils such as spoons, spatulas and the like. Where possible, especially with utensils, keep just one or, at a push, two of each. No one truly needs two balloon whisks or several slotted spoons.

I think a full set of pans only needs to consist of three varying sized saucepans with lids – including a really big one for pasta. Plus a large non-stick frying pan and a wok or large sauté pan. Buy the best you can afford, treat with care and your pans will last you for years.

When it comes to tins for baking, always choose non-stick. For cake and tart tins, go for the springform, loose-bottomed variety as they make it much easier to get your cakes and tarts out in one piece. For muffins and individual tarts, look out for ovenproof rubber moulds – as they are flexible, the tarts simply pop out. And make sure you buy sturdy roasting tins and baking sheets – inexpensive, thin baking sheets are liable to buckle in the oven.

Electrical items

All electrical kitchen goods are designed to make your life easier. Although you can manage without them, for example by using a mouli grinder in place of a hand-held blender, or a pestle and mortar or heavy knife in place of a mini chopper, most small electrical items are reasonably priced and though they may have a relatively short life, the time they save is invaluable.

Weighing scales It's essential to have an accurate set of kitchen scales, be they electronic, spring-operated or balance scales.

Electric mixer A hand-held electric mixer really does save a lot of time as well as tiring wrist-action. I wouldn't fancy making my snowy saffron peaches (page 184) without mine. This appliance is inexpensive and easy to clean.

Hand-held blender My wand or stick blender is always on the go for smoothing out sauces and soups. It's a lot safer and easier than pouring batches of very hot soup into the goblet of a free-standing electric blender on the worktop.

Small food processor Okay, so you might not use all the fancy blades but it's fantastic for whizzing up pastry and fine chopping work. If you don't think you'd use it enough, save your cash and instead invest in a mini chopper.

Mini chopper My single most invaluable piece of electrical equipment, this gets used several times a week in my kitchen. It's ideal for chopping small quantities and whizzing up pestos and salsas. A mini chopper is pretty inexpensive, but because the blade is small it does become blunt after extensive use.

Electrical juicer This is one of the most used items of equipment in my kitchen. It works by centrifugal force and the high-speed spin separates out the pulp and delivers you delicious, vitamin-packed juice. The most hi-tech versions extract the maximum juice possible from the fruit but they are very expensive. My cheaper version, though stained and a little dented, still works well after five years of vigorous usage.

1 breakfasts

raspberry granola

This is way tastier than any shop-bought oaty cereal and can be stored in an airtight container for about a fortnight. I like to serve it with fresh raspberries, but it's also good with other fruit such as sliced banana or ready-to-eat dried apricots.
Illustrated left

SERVES 12

200g (7oz) jumbo porridge oats
75g (3oz) desiccated coconut
150g (5oz) pecan nuts, roughly chopped
1/2 teaspoon ground cinnamon
1 tablespoon sunflower oil

75g (3oz) butter, melted
75g (3oz) light muscovado sugar
3 tablespoons maple syrup

TO SERVE:
semi-skimmed milk or Greek yogurt
raspberries or other fruit

1 Preheat the oven to 170°C (fan oven 150°C), gas mark 3. Mix all the ingredients together and spread out on a large baking tray, leaving some of the mixture in clumps. Bake for 30–35 minutes until golden and crunchy.

2 Remove the granola from the oven and leave to cool, then break up into clumps. Serve in bowls with milk or yogurt and fresh raspberries.

potted fruity muesli yogurt

You need to remember to put this together before you go to bed if you plan to eat it for breakfast the next day, but it takes only a few minutes to prepare. During the hours in the fridge the muesli softens in the yogurt. I love to use pineapple but you can try it with pretty well any fruit. The granola (above) makes a good alternative to the muesli.

SERVES 4

6 tablespoons Swiss style muesli
2 fresh pineapple rings, drained and
  roughly chopped
2 x 150g (5oz) cartons apricot yogurt
4 tablespoons milk

1 Spoon the muesli into four small bowls or large ramekins. Sprinkle over the chopped pineapple. Mix the yogurt with the milk, then spoon over the fruit. Cover the bowls with cling film and chill in the refrigerator overnight.

2 The next morning, stir the muesli yogurt well and serve.

banana, apricot and orange blitz

Get the day off to the right start with a glass of this gorgeous tipple.
Illustrated right

SERVES 2

2 bananas

8 ready-to-eat dried apricots, roughly chopped

300–400ml (10–14fl oz) freshly squeezed orange juice

1   Peel the bananas, break into pieces and put in a blender. Add the apricots and a splash of the orange juice and whiz until smooth. Add the remaining juice and whiz again until thick and frothy. Pour into glasses and drink straightaway.

strawberry booster

Don't be put off by the name – believe me this is delicious and it will certainly send you off to work with a spring in your step.
Illustrated far right

SERVES 1

100g (3¹/₂oz) strawberries, hulled and halved

1–2 tablespoons thin honey

1 tablespoon wheatgerm

100ml (3¹/₂fl oz) milk

1   Place the strawberries, honey, wheatgerm and a splash of milk in a blender and whiz until smooth. Add the remaining milk and whiz again until thick and frothy. Pour into a glass and drink straightaway.

mango lassi

A classic lassi is simply yogurt, water and either sugar or salt, to taste. This one is bolstered with fresh mango and apple juice and makes a refreshing start to the day.

SERVES 2

1 large ripe mango, peeled, stoned and diced

150g (5oz) natural yogurt

150ml (¹/₄ pint) freshly pressed apple juice

1   Place the mango in a food processor or blender and whiz to a smooth purée. Add the yogurt and apple juice and whiz again until smooth and frothy. Pour into ice-filled glasses and serve.

cinnamon pancakes

Hot pancakes straight from the pan with some sliced banana and a drizzle of honey make a fantastic breakfast. These are thin pancakes so a little batter goes quite a long way: if you have any pancakes left over, layer them up with greaseproof paper and freeze.

SERVES 4–6

125g (4oz) plain flour
2 teaspoons ground cinnamon
pinch of salt
1 egg
300ml (½ pint) milk

sunflower oil, for frying

TO SERVE:
4 large bananas
thin honey or maple syrup, to drizzle

1 Sift the flour, cinnamon and salt into a large bowl. Make a well in the centre and crack in the egg. Using a balloon whisk, gradually beat in the milk to make a smooth batter. If you have time, leave it to rest in the fridge for 30 minutes.

2 Heat a 20cm (8 inch) pancake pan or non-stick frying pan. Add a few drops of oil and, when hot but not smoking, ladle in some batter. Quickly swirl to cover the bottom of the pan thinly. Cook for a minute or so on each side, then slide on to a plate. Repeat with the remaining batter to make at least 12 pancakes.

3 If you want to cook a few pancakes before starting to serve them, stack them up with a square of greaseproof paper between each one.

4 Serve the pancakes as soon as you can. Peel and slice the bananas. Place the pancakes on warm plates, fold them over and top with the sliced bananas. Drizzle with honey or maple syrup and serve.

breakfast breads

For thousands of years, bread has been a staple food and its wonderful versatility has made it the base, or companion, for most of our meals. And whether it's first thing in the morning or last thing at night, bread is one of the first things we reach for when we need food in a hurry. After all, what can be more instantly satisfying than hot buttered toast and homemade jam?

Over the past few years, the variety of breads in our supermarkets has increased dramatically, with a choice of Italian breads such as ciabatta and focaccia, flatbreads from the Middle East, rustic French breads, bagels, pittas and soda farls now available alongside our traditional breads. And as the range increases, the shelf life of many breads is also extending. Many special purpose breads, such as naan and flour tortillas, are vacuum packed and last for weeks, and all bread freezes brilliantly. Try the following original breakfast ideas; each serves 4.

▲ **vanilla eggy bread**
Lightly whisk 4 large eggs with 4 tbsp double cream in a shallow dish. Dip 8 slices of day-old white bread into the mixture and turn to coat. Heat 2 tbsp sunflower oil in a large frying pan and fry the eggy bread slices, two or three at a time, for 2–3 minutes on each side until golden. Remove and keep warm while you cook the rest. Sprinkle each slice of eggy bread with vanilla caster sugar and serve with sliced peaches or other fresh fruit and a spoonful of yogurt.

sausage, onion and mustard soda farls

Cook 8 Toulouse or other pork sausages on a hot griddle pan, turning, until browned and cooked through; remove and keep warm. Fry 1 sliced large onion on the griddle for 4 minutes, sprinkling over a little salt and olive oil. Split 4 soda farls open to make pockets. Halve the sausages and put into the farls with the onion, a little American mustard and seasoning; press well. Toast on the griddle for 2–3 minutes each side.

English breakfast salad

Grill 8 rashers of smoked dry-cured streaky bacon until golden and crisp; break into pieces. Tear ½ ciabatta loaf into bite-sized pieces and fry in 2 tbsp olive oil for 3–4 minutes, until crisp and golden; drain on kitchen paper. Divide the bacon, ciabatta croûtons and some rocket leaves between four plates. Poach 4 eggs in simmering water for 4–5 minutes, remove and place on the salad. Whisk 3 tbsp olive oil with 1 tbsp balsamic vinegar and seasoning. Drizzle over the salad and serve.

▲ mozzarella and tomato bagel melt

Preheat the oven to 190°C, gas 5. Split 4 plain bagels in half horizontally. Arrange sliced mozzarella and sliced ripe tomatoes over the bases. Scatter a few basil leaves on top, drizzle with a little olive oil and season with salt and pepper. Press the other halves of the bagels on top to make sandwiches. Place on a baking sheet and bake in the oven for 15–20 minutes until the cheese has melted and the bagels are crisp and golden.

chorizo omelette

Chorizo is fantastic in an omelette – for this I always use the pre-sliced variety. Keep the omelette nice and light – don't be tempted to beat the eggs with milk rather than water.

SERVES 1

8 chorizo sausage slices, each roughly torn in
 half
1 garlic clove, peeled and thinly sliced
2 eggs

1 tablespoon very roughly chopped
 flat leaf parsley
sea salt and freshly ground black pepper
Tabasco, to serve

1 Heat a large non-stick frying pan. Add the chorizo slices and cook for 2 minutes, then toss in the garlic slices.

2 Meanwhile, crack the eggs into a bowl. Using a fork, whisk with 2 tablespoons of water and plenty of seasoning, then stir in the chopped parsley.

3 Pour the egg mixture into the pan and cook over a high heat for a couple of minutes, tilting the pan to swirl the egg, until golden and set. Flip over and cook the other side for 1 minute. Slide on to a warm plate and serve with some Tabasco for shaking over, and hot buttered toast if you like.

Parmesan baked eggs and mushrooms

Because the cream runs and the cheese melts, I recommend you bake these in individual dishes. Serve with hot buttered toast.

SERVES 4

50g (2oz) butter, at room temperature
2 garlic cloves, peeled and crushed
2 tablespoons chopped chives or flat leaf parsley
4 large field mushrooms

4 small eggs
6–8 tablespoons double cream
4 tablespoons freshly grated Parmesan cheese
sea salt and freshly ground black pepper

1 Preheat the oven to 180°C (fan oven 160°C), gas mark 4. Mix together the butter, garlic and chives. Cut the stalk out of each mushroom and place the caps, gill-side up, in individual heatproof dishes. Season with salt and pepper and dot over the herb butter. Bake for 15 minutes until softened.

2 Carefully crack an egg into each mushroom cap. Swirl a tablespoon or two of cream over each egg and season with salt and pepper, then sprinkle with grated Parmesan. Bake for 6–8 minutes until the egg is just set, then serve.

pancetta potato cakes

An Italian-influenced hash brown, this is perfect as an on-the-way-out-of-the-door bite. If you have a little more time, top with a poached egg for a scrumptious weekend brunch.

SERVES 4

4 medium floury potatoes, such as Maris Piper
or King Edward, about 800g (1 3/4 lb) in total,
scrubbed
125g (4 oz) cubed pancetta
1 shallot, peeled and finely chopped
1 tablespoon vegetable oil (if needed)
sea salt and freshly ground black pepper

1 Cook the whole potatoes in a pan of boiling salted water for 15 minutes.

2 Meanwhile, heat a large non-stick frying pan and add the pancetta. Cook for 3–4 minutes, then add the shallot and cook for a few minutes more until it has softened and the pancetta is crisp and golden. Using a slotted spoon, transfer the pancetta and shallot to a large bowl.

3 Drain the potatoes. When they are cool enough to handle, coarsely grate them into the bowl. Add some salt and pepper and mix well together. Firmly shape the mixture in the palm of the hands into eight small ovals.

4 Using the same pan, fry the potato cakes for 3–4 minutes on each side until crisp and golden brown. There should be enough fat left in the pan from the pancetta, but if not add a splash of oil.

5 Drain the crisp potato cakes on kitchen paper and serve while still hot.

Italian fried eggs

A fried egg is a very personal thing. For me, the key is a good crispy base, but feel free to cook yours the way you like it.

SERVES 1

1 plum tomato, thickly sliced
1 thick slice of ciabatta or other rustic bread
2 tablespoons olive oil
1 large egg
1 small garlic clove, peeled and thinly sliced
1/2 small red chilli, thinly sliced (optional)
large handful of snipped chives
1/2 teaspoon balsamic vinegar
sea salt and freshly ground black pepper

1 Heat a ridged cast-iron griddle pan. Lightly brush the tomato slices and bread with a little olive oil. Cook the tomato slices first, for at least 5 minutes. When they're nearly ready, toast the bread in the same pan until nicely bar-marked.

2 In the meantime, pour a little olive oil into a small non-stick frying pan and crack in the egg. After a minute or so add the garlic, and chilli if using. Cook for a further couple of minutes, spooning the hot oil over the egg until it is cooked to your liking.

3 Place the griddled bread on a plate and quickly spoon the tomatoes on top.

4 Throw the chives into the egg pan and splash in the balsamic vinegar. Season generously, then slide the egg on to the tomatoes and drizzle over the pan juices. Serve straightaway, with a good cup of tea.

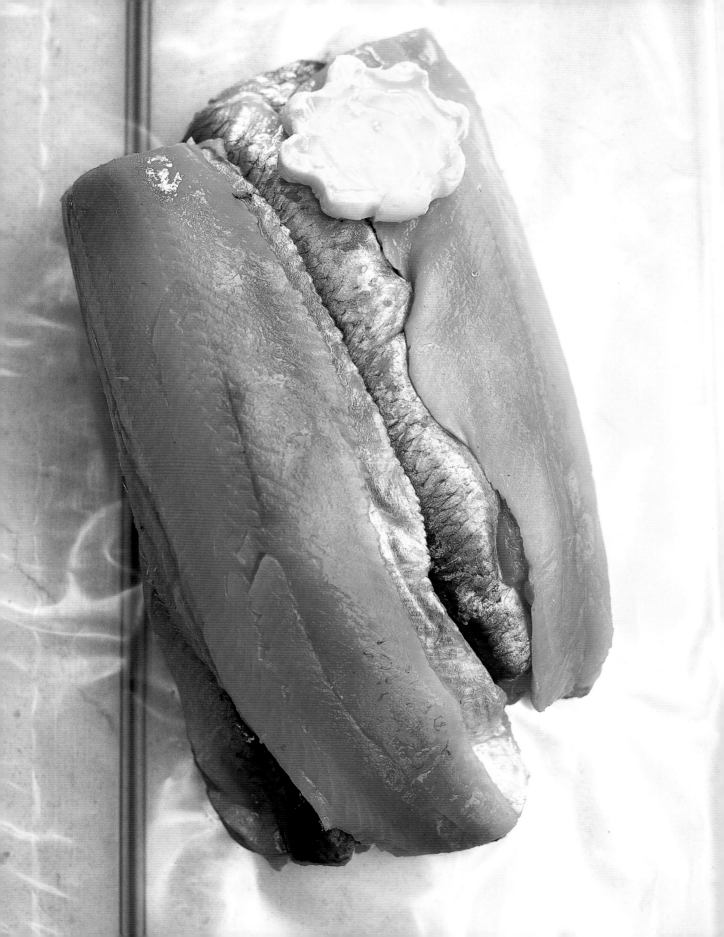

kipper and boiled egg hash

This is a speedy spin on that all-time brilliant breakfast, kedgeree. I'm a real fan of boil-in-the-bag kippers. It means I get to eat them without being reminded of it for the rest of the week each time I turn the grill on! I always add the buttery juices from inside the bag too.
Illustrated on previous page

SERVES 4
230g packet boil-in-the-bag kippers
6 eggs
2 large red-skinned potatoes, such as Desirée,
*   about 500g (1lb 2oz) in total, peeled*
*   and grated*
2 tablespoons olive oil
1 garlic clove, peeled and finely chopped
1 tablespoon cumin seeds, roughly crushed
1 teaspoon dried chilli flakes
1 bunch of spring onions, trimmed and sliced
small bunch of coriander, roughly chopped
sea salt and freshly ground black pepper
lemon or lime wedges, to serve

1 Put the bag of kippers and the eggs into a pan of boiling water and cook for 8 minutes.

2 Meanwhile, thoroughly rinse the grated potatoes and squeeze out as much liquid as possible. Heat the olive oil in a large frying pan and add the potatoes. Season with salt and pepper and cook for 10–12 minutes over a low heat, stirring occasionally. Add the garlic, cumin and chilli flakes, and cook for a further 1 minute.

3 Drain the kippers and eggs. Cool the eggs under cold running water, then shell and roughly chop them. Open the kipper bag and carefully pour the juices into the potatoes in the frying pan.

4 Roughly flake the kipper flesh with a fork and add to the pan together with the eggs and spring onions. Mix well and heat through gently for 2–3 minutes. Stir in the chopped coriander and serve, with lemon or lime wedges.

ham and cheese puffs

These are best eaten hot, straight from the oven, but if you have a pop-up toaster that can take wide toasted sandwiches, you can use it to reheat them. Alternatively, wrap in greaseproof paper and pop into your lunchbox.

MAKES 4

375g packet ready rolled puff pastry
1 tablespoon Dijon mustard
200g (7oz) Gruyère, Emmental or Jarslberg
  cheese, thinly sliced
50g (2oz) wafer thin ham, roughly torn
25g (1oz) butter, melted

1 Preheat the oven to 200°C (fan oven 180°C), gas mark 6. Roll out the puff pastry to a 30 x 44cm (12 x 17½ inch) rectangle. Cut into eight 15 x 11cm (6 x 4½ inch) rectangles.

2 Spread four of the rectangles with the mustard, then cover with the cheese, taking the slices right up to the edges. Scatter over the ham. Place the other four rectangles of puff pastry on top and press down firmly. Squeeze the edges of each tart together between the thumb and forefinger to seal.

3 Arrange the tarts on a baking sheet lined with silicone paper and brush them with melted butter. Bake for 20 minutes until dark golden. The cheese will ooze out around the edges but don't worry.

4 Lift the tarts off the paper and cool slightly for a few minutes before serving. Alternatively, allow to cool and reheat in the toaster.

2 everyday suppers

spaghetti with mussels

Every time I make this dish – and as anyone who knows me will tell you, that's incredibly often – I'm amazed how quick, simple and tasty it is. In fact, it is so quick, it's always ready before the table is even laid!

SERVES 4

1kg (2 ¼ lb) fresh mussels
300g (11oz) dried spaghetti
150ml (¼ pint) dry white wine
2 garlic cloves, peeled and finely chopped
1 red chilli, deseeded and finely chopped
2 tablespoons chopped parsley
sea salt and freshly ground black pepper
olive oil, to serve

1 Discard any broken mussels, and those that do not close when sharply tapped. Scrub the mussels thoroughly in cold water and pull out the little beards.

2 Cook the spaghetti in a large pan of boiling salted water according to the packet instructions until *al dente* (tender, but firm to the bite).

3 Meanwhile, combine the white wine, garlic, chilli and some pepper in a large pan. Bring to the boil and simmer rapidly for 5 minutes. Add the mussels to the pan, cover tightly and cook for 5 minutes, shaking the pan from time to time, until all the shells have opened; discard any that don't.

4 Drain the pasta and return to the pan. Add the parsley and the mussel mixture, and toss well together. Divide among four warm bowls and drizzle a splash of olive oil over each serving.

butter-roasted cod with spring onion mash

The tricky thing about cooking skinless fish is preventing it flaking apart as you serve it. Cooking it this way, on sheets of greaseproof paper, means you can slide the fish on to the plate without it breaking. The soft spring onion mash makes a perfect partner.

SERVES 6

2kg (4½lb) floury potatoes, such as Maris Piper
  or King Edward, peeled and cubed
6 skinless cod fillet pieces, each about 150g (5oz)
large knob of butter, plus extra to grease

grated zest and juice of 1 lime
2 bunches of spring onions, trimmed and
  thinly sliced
4–5 tablespoons olive oil
sea salt and freshly ground black pepper

1 Preheat the oven to 220°C (fan oven 200°C), gas mark 7. Cook the potatoes in a large pan of boiling salted water for 15–20 minutes until tender.

2 Meanwhile, cut out six rectangles of greaseproof paper just large enough to sit a piece of fish on. Lightly butter each piece of paper and place on a large baking sheet. Put the fish on the paper and dot with butter. Sprinkle the lime zest over the fish and season with salt and pepper.

3 When the potatoes are almost cooked, pop the fish into the oven and roast for 6–8 minutes, depending on thickness, until just cooked.

4 Drain the potatoes well and return to the pan. Mash roughly with a fork, then stir in the lime juice, spring onions and olive oil. Season to taste.

5 Divide the flavoured mash among warm serving plates. Gently ease each piece of fish off the paper and slide on top of the mash. Serve immediately.

special fish curry

Though very easy, this is a really stylish supper dish – certainly smart enough to serve for a midweek dinner party. The coconut, limes and ginger will tickle tastebuds you never knew you had! Serve with basmati or jasmine rice and mini poppadoms.

Illustrated on previous page

SERVES 6

1 tablespoon sunflower oil
1 large onion, peeled and finely chopped
2 garlic cloves, peeled and finely chopped
5cm (2 inch) piece of fresh root ginger, peeled
  and finely chopped
2 tablespoons hot curry paste
300ml (1/2 pint) chicken stock
400ml can coconut milk
2 teaspoons caster sugar
1/4 teaspoon salt
750g (1lb 10oz) skinless white fish fillet, such as
  coley, pollack, haddock, cod or monkfish, cut
  into large chunks
400g (14oz) peeled raw tiger prawns, thawed
  if frozen
juice of 2 limes, or to taste
small handful of coriander leaves, to serve

1 Heat the oil in a large sauté pan and cook the onion, garlic and ginger for 5 minutes until softened. Stir in the curry paste and cook for 2 minutes. Add the chicken stock and coconut milk and bring to a gentle simmer (do not boil as the coconut milk could separate).

2 Stir in the sugar and salt, then add the fish. Simmer for just 2 minutes or so until the fish is opaque, then add the prawns and cook for 1–2 minutes until pink.

3 Add lime juice to taste, then ladle the curry into warm bowls. Scatter over the coriander to serve.

haddock and coriander fish cakes

I think this dish offers the best of both worlds – the warm, fluffy potato and brilliant, flaky haddock from our coastline with the red curry kick and fragrant coriander of Thailand.

SERVES 4

1kg (2¼ lb) floury potatoes, such as Maris Piper
  or King Edward, peeled and diced
400g (14oz) haddock fillet
300ml (½ pint) milk
1 tablespoon Thai red curry paste
1 bunch of spring onions, trimmed and
  thinly sliced
4 tablespoons chopped coriander
4 tablespoons plain flour, seasoned
1 egg, beaten
75g (3oz) natural or golden dried breadcrumbs
2–3 tablespoons sunflower oil
sea salt and freshly ground black pepper
2 limes, cut into wedges, to serve

1 Cook the potatoes in a large pan of boiling water for 15 minutes or so until tender.

2 Meanwhile, place the fish in a large sauté pan and pour over the milk. Cover and bring to the boil, then immediately remove from the heat and leave the fish to cook in the residual heat for 5 minutes, or until it can be flaked.

3 Drain the potatoes well and return to the pan. Mash until smooth, then stir in the curry paste, spring onions and chopped coriander.

4 Drain the fish well. Flake roughly, discarding any skin and bones, then lightly stir into the mash mixture. Season with salt and pepper to taste. Shape the mixture into eight cakes, patting to compact them. If you have time, cover and chill so the cakes firm up.

5 Dust the fish cakes in the seasoned flour, then carefully dip them in the beaten egg, then into the breadcrumbs to coat on all sides. Heat the oil in a heavy-based frying pan and shallow-fry the fish cakes in batches for 2 minutes on each side until crisp and golden. Drain on kitchen paper and serve, with lime wedges.

quick grilled mackerel with lemon mint drizzle

Mackerel is a wonderful fish – it's packed with all the right kinds of oils and is really economical too. These fillets are cooked under a hot grill and are ready in just a few minutes. Serve with a simple leafy salad and some boiled new potatoes for a satisfying, healthy family meal.

SERVES 4

4 whole mackerel, each about 300g (11oz),
 filleted
1 small garlic clove, peeled and quartered
3 spring onions, trimmed and roughly chopped
20g (3/4 oz) mint
1 small lemon
1 tablespoon capers, drained and rinsed
4 tablespoons extra virgin olive oil
sea salt and freshly ground black pepper

1   Preheat the grill to high. Season the mackerel fillets, then arrange skin-side up on a foil-lined baking sheet. Cook under the grill for 3 minutes on each side.

2   Meanwhile, put the garlic and spring onions in a small food processor and whiz until finely chopped. Tear in the mint leaves, grate in the lemon zest, and add the capers and a little salt. Whiz again. Squeeze in the juice from half the lemon and pour in the olive oil, then give one final blitz to blend thoroughly.

3   Place the grilled mackerel on warm serving plates and drizzle over the dressing. Serve immediately.

spiced chicken with herb cous cous

I went to Egypt on holiday recently and ate a version of this at a local restaurant two or three times. I loved the crispy, succulent chicken. It's so easy to make I now knock it up at home too!

SERVES 4

4 chicken breasts, each about 125g (4oz)
2–3 teaspoons harissa or other thick chilli paste
300g (11oz) cous cous
1 red onion, peeled and finely chopped
350ml (12fl oz) hot chicken stock
grated zest and juice of 1 lemon

2 ripe tomatoes, roughly chopped
200g (7oz) feta cheese, crumbled into small pieces
20g (³⁄₄oz) parsley, roughly chopped
20g (³⁄₄oz) coriander, roughly chopped
3 tablespoons olive oil
sea salt and freshly ground black pepper
1 lime, cut into wedges, to serve

1 Preheat the grill to medium. Deeply slash the skin side of the chicken, then rub the harissa into each breast, making sure it goes into the slashes.

2 Arrange the chicken skin-side down on a foil-lined grill pan. Cook under the grill for 6–7 minutes on each side or until cooked through with a crisp skin.

3 Meanwhile, place the cous cous and red onion in a large heatproof bowl and pour over the hot stock and the lemon juice. Leave to soak for 10 minutes until all the liquid has been absorbed.

4 Break up the cous cous with a fork, then stir through the tomatoes, feta, lemon zest, herbs and olive oil. Add salt and pepper to taste.

5 Place the chicken and warm cous cous on warm plates and add a lime wedge on the side.

chicken vindaloo

Vindaloo is traditionally associated with Goa but its origins are actually in Portugal, with the 'vin' part of the name meaning wine. It is classically made with pork and always with a wet curry paste. This simplified version uses chicken thighs and a jar of vindaloo curry paste. Serve with basmati rice and some simple greens.

SERVES 4

8 skinless chicken thigh fillets, about
  900g (2lb) in total, cubed
3 tablespoons vindaloo curry paste
1–2 tablespoons sunflower oil
1 onion, peeled and chopped
10cm (4 inch) piece of fresh root ginger, peeled
  and chopped
150ml (¼ pint) dry white wine
300ml (½ pint) hot chicken stock
1 teaspoon dark soft brown sugar
sea salt and freshly ground black pepper
1 mild green chilli, thinly sliced, to garnish

1 Place the chicken cubes in a bowl, add the curry paste and turn to coat. Leave to marinate in the fridge for at least 30 minutes, or up to 8 hours.

2 Heat the oil in a large pan and cook the chicken for 3–4 minutes. Add the onion and ginger and cook for a further 5 minutes until golden.

3 Pour in the wine and bubble rapidly for 5 minutes until it evaporates, then stir in the stock and brown sugar. Bring to the boil and simmer gently for 20 minutes. Season with salt and pepper to taste.

4 Divide the curry among warm plates and scatter over the sliced chilli to serve.

lamb and red onion pilaf

The sweetness of red onions and lamb is even more delicious when matched with the savoury flavours of cumin and coriander. The chilli kick is warm rather than hot, so this pilaf is fine for all ages. Serve with a leafy salad.

SERVES 4

2–3 tablespoons sunflower oil

2 tablespoons plain flour

1 teaspoon ground cumin

1/2 teaspoon ground coriander

1 teaspoon hot chilli powder

750g (1lb 10oz) boneless lamb, cubed

2 red onions, peeled and thickly sliced

2 garlic cloves, peeled and thinly sliced

1 red chilli, deseeded and finely chopped

400g (14oz) basmati rice

750ml (1¼ pints) hot vegetable stock

1 tablespoon hot curry paste

juice of 1 lemon

sea salt and freshly ground black pepper

20g (¾oz) coriander, to serve

1   Pour 2 tablespoons of the oil into a large flameproof casserole and set it over a medium heat. Meanwhile, stir together the flour, cumin, coriander, chilli powder and some salt and pepper.

2   Toss the lamb cubes in the flour mixture, then fry in the hot oil for 5 minutes until nicely browned (you may have to do this in two batches). Remove the lamb with a slotted spoon and set aside.

3   If the pan is dry, add another tablespoon of oil, then cook the onions for 5 minutes. Stir in the garlic and fresh chilli and cook for a further 1 minute.

4   Stir in the rice and return the lamb to the casserole, then pour over the stock. Mix in the curry paste, using a wooden spoon to scrape up all the tasty bits from the bottom of the pan, and bring to the boil. Reduce the heat, cover and simmer gently for 15 minutes until the rice is tender and all the liquid has been absorbed.

5   Stir in the lemon juice and check the seasoning. Divide among warm plates and scatter a few coriander leaves over each serving.

spiced lamb koftas with tzatziki

This is a classic Greek-style kebab, served in traditional style with tzatziki, pitta bread and salad. It will be on the table in the time it would take to wait for your order in a local Greek taverna. *Illustrated on previous page*

SERVES 4

500g (1lb 2oz) lean lamb mince
1 small onion, peeled and finely chopped
3 tablespoons chopped mint
1 tablespoon chopped oregano
1 teaspoon ground coriander
1/2 small cucumber
150g (5oz) natural yogurt
1 garlic clove, peeled and crushed
1 lemon, cut into 6 wedges
sea salt and freshly ground black pepper
TO SERVE:
4 pitta breads
salad leaves, such as baby spinach or rocket
small mint leaves

1 Soak 12 wooden skewers in hot water for 10 minutes. Preheat the grill to high. Mix together the lamb, onion, 2 tablespoons of the mint, the oregano, coriander and a seasoning of salt and pepper.

2 Divide the mixture into 12 portions and squeeze around the pre-soaked skewers. Grill the lamb kebabs for 8–10 minutes, turning occasionally, until well browned and cooked through.

3 Meanwhile, grate the cucumber and squeeze out the excess liquid with your hands. Mix with the yogurt, garlic and remaining mint. Add some salt and squeeze in the juice from one or two of the lemon wedges.

4 Warm the pitta breads under the grill, turning once. Serve the lamb kebabs in the warm pittas, with the salad leaves, tzatziki and mint leaves. Accompany with the remaining lemon wedges.

barbecued lamb leg steaks with summer salad

I can't tell you how many times I've made this, but on warm, summer evenings when the aromas of rosemary and mint start filling the garden, it's the first choice for the barbecue. Serve with warmed pitta breads or flour tortillas.

SERVES 6

3 tablespoons plain flour
1 tablespoon dried oregano
1 teaspoon dried rosemary
1 teaspoon salt
1 teaspoon steak pepper or coarsely cracked
  black peppercorns
1 teaspoon cayenne pepper
6 lamb leg steaks, bone in, each about 150g (5oz)
1 tablespoon sunflower oil (if using a griddle pan)

FOR THE SALAD:

1 cucumber, peeled and cubed
1 small red onion, peeled and thinly sliced
6 ripe tomatoes
2 tablespoons red wine vinegar
3 tablespoons olive oil
60g (2¼oz) wild rocket
20g (¾oz) mint
sea salt and freshly ground black pepper

1 Mix together the flour, oregano, rosemary, salt, pepper and cayenne. Lightly dust the lamb leg steaks in the flour mixture. Cook over a barbecue fire, or in a lightly oiled very hot griddle pan, for 3–5 minutes on each side until nicely browned but still slightly pink in the centre.

2 To make the salad, combine the cucumber and red onion in a large serving bowl. Halve each tomato horizontally, then cut each half into four. Add to the bowl with the vinegar, olive oil and rocket. Tear in the mint leaves and season with salt and pepper to taste. Toss gently together.

3 Place the lamb steaks on serving plates. Place the salad and a pile of pitta breads or flour tortillas in the centre of the table so everyone can help themselves.

Vietnamese beef noodles

This is a modern twist on classic Vietnamese street food, with a clean-flavoured, citrusy stock and lots of crunchy vegetables. It's one of my all-time favourite quick suppers.

SERVES 4

3 x 150g packets vacuum-packed straight-to-wok
thin noodles
200g (7oz) mixed baby corn and mangetout
200g (7oz) small pak choi
1.2 litres (2 pints) hot chicken stock
4cm (1½ inch) piece of fresh root ginger, peeled
and cut into matchsticks

350g (12oz) very thin steaks (sandwich or
minute steaks)
1 tablespoon chilli sauce
2–3 tablespoons soy sauce
juice of 2 limes, or to taste
150g (5oz) bean sprouts
handful of coriander leaves

1   Place the noodles in a heatproof bowl and pour over boiling water to cover. Set aside.

2   Halve the baby corn and pak choi lengthways. Pour the stock into a large pan, add the ginger and bring to the boil.

3   Meanwhile, heat a non-stick griddle pan until very hot. Brush the steaks with the chilli sauce, then place on the hot griddle pan and cook for 1 minute on each side. Transfer to a plate and set aside to rest for a couple of minutes.

4   Add the baby corn, mangetout and pak choi to the stock, return to a simmer and cook for about 2 minutes until just tender. Stir in the soy sauce and lime juice to taste.

5   Drain the noodles and divide among four warm bowls. Add the bean sprouts and ladle the stock on top. Thinly slice the steaks and add to the bowls. Scatter coriander leaves over and serve.

dill pickle cheese burgers

I always seem to end up making these whenever my nephews come to visit. I don't know whether it's the crunchy pickles, or the melting cheese or the lovely juicy burgers, but the plates always come back clean. If you want to spice up the burgers, whiz one or two deseeded red chillies with the bread and parsley.

SERVES 6

2 slices of white bread, crusts removed
20g (3/4oz) flat leaf parsley, roughly chopped
1 egg
750g (1lb 10oz) lean beef mince
2 dill pickles, finely chopped, or 2 tablespoons
   chopped gherkins
sea salt and freshly ground black pepper

TO SERVE:

6 crusty buns, or burger buns
6 slices Port Salut, Jarlsberg or Cheddar cheese
tomato ketchup to taste (optional)

1 Tear the white bread into pieces and place in a food processor with the parsley. Whiz until the bread is broken into crumbs. Transfer to a large bowl.

2 Using a wooden spoon, mix in the egg, beef, pickles and plenty of salt and pepper. You may need to use your hands to work the mixture together.

3 Preheat a griddle pan or the grill. Shape the mixture into eight even-sized burgers that are no more than 1cm (1/2 inch) thick. Cook on the griddle pan, or under the grill, for 3–4 minutes on each side until nicely browned and cooked to your taste.

4 Split open the buns and place a burger on the bottom of each. Top with a slice of cheese and a squirt of tomato ketchup if you like, then put on the lid and serve with salad.

stir-fried steak chilli

This is a guaranteed winner in my house and it's incredibly quick to make – about 15 minutes from shopping bag to table. My friend Angela adds a shot of espresso coffee to her chilli – it imparts a real depth of flavour. If you want to try this trick, add it with the fruity sauce.

SERVES 4

1 tablespoon vegetable oil

500g (1lb 2oz) rump steak, cubed

1 bunch of spring onions, trimmed and
   thickly sliced

4 mild green chillies, deseeded and roughly
   chopped

1 teaspoon cumin seeds

1 teaspoon cayenne pepper or hot chilli powder

4 ripe tomatoes, roughly chopped

410g can cannellini beans, drained

1 tablespoon fruity brown sauce

2 tablespoons roughly chopped flat leaf parsley

sea salt and freshly ground black pepper

TO SERVE:

150ml ($^1/_4$ pint) soured cream

150ml ($^1/_4$ pint) fresh guacamole

175g (6oz) tortilla chips

1   Heat a wok, add the oil and when it is very hot, add the steak. Stir-fry for 2–3 minutes until starting to brown. Add the onions, chillies, cumin seeds and cayenne and stir-fry for another 2 minutes.

2   Lower the heat and stir in the tomatoes, then cook over a high heat for a couple of minutes until they begin to soften. Add the cannellini beans and fruity sauce, and simmer gently for a further 5 minutes until piping hot. Season with salt and pepper to taste, and stir in the parsley.

3   Serve the chilli with plain boiled rice and pass round the soured cream, guacamole and tortilla chips.

pan-fried pork chops with rosemary and spinach

When it comes to pork, I always say, take it nice and slow. When I've rubbed the chops with oil and seasoning, I cook them really gently until they're beautifully golden but still tender and moist. Serve this with mashed potato.

SERVES 4

4 pork chops, each about 175g (6oz)
4 long rosemary sprigs
1 tablespoon olive oil
1kg (2¼lb) leaf spinach, washed
small knob of butter
1 garlic clove, peeled and thinly sliced
sea salt and freshly ground black pepper

1 Push a metal skewer horizontally through each chop and remove, then push the rosemary sprig through each hole. Rub the chops with olive oil and season with salt and pepper.

2 Preheat a non-stick frying pan and gently cook the chops for 15–20 minutes until nicely browned and cooked through.

3 Meanwhile, cram the spinach into a large pan, cover with a tight-fitting lid and cook gently for 5 minutes until wilted. Tip into a colander and press with a wooden spoon to extract the excess water.

4 Transfer the pork chops to a warm plate and set aside in a warm spot to rest for 5 minutes.

5 Add the butter to the hot frying pan, then toss in the garlic and cook for a minute or so. Add the wilted spinach and some seasoning and cook gently for 4–5 minutes, stirring from time to time.

6 Serve the chops with the soft spinach, and with any juices from the pork spooned over.

fusilli with Savoy cabbage and crispy bacon

Definitely delicious, this one's a real winner when you're feeling a bit strapped for cash. I like to eat it from a bowl in front of the television when the rain is pouring down outside.

SERVES 4

500g (1lb 2oz) dried fusilli or other pasta shapes
½ Savoy cabbage, thinly sliced
6 rashers of dry-cured streaky bacon
2 tablespoons olive oil
1 onion, peeled and finely chopped
2 garlic cloves, peeled and thinly sliced
2 red chillies, halved, deseeded and thinly sliced
6 tablespoons freshly grated Parmesan cheese,
  plus extra to serve
sea salt and freshly ground black pepper

1 Cook the pasta in a large pan of boiling salted water according to the packet instructions until *al dente* (tender, but firm to the bite). About 5 minutes before the pasta is due to finish cooking, add the cabbage to the pan.

2 Meanwhile, cut the bacon rashers across into 1cm (½ inch) strips. Heat the olive oil in a frying pan and cook the bacon for 1–2 minutes. Add the onion, garlic and chillies and cook for a further 5 minutes until the onion has softened.

3 Drain the pasta and cabbage well and return to the pan. Season the bacon mixture with a little salt and plenty of pepper, then stir into the pasta and cabbage. Sprinkle in the Parmesan and toss together. Divide among warm bowls and serve immediately, with more grated Parmesan for passing round.

sausage piece penne

This is a real heart-warming dish. I use Lincolnshire sausages because I love their subtle spicing, but any quality pork sausages would do. To turn this into a warming winter bake, transfer to an ovenproof dish, sprinkle with grated Parmesan and bake at 200°C (fan oven 180°C), gas mark 6 for 30 minutes until the top is crusty and golden brown.

SERVES 6

900g (2lb) Lincolnshire pork sausages
2 onions, peeled and chopped
4 garlic cloves, peeled and chopped
2 red chillies, deseeded and finely chopped
3 sage sprigs
2 x 400g cans chopped tomatoes
1 teaspoon soft brown sugar
500g (1lb 2oz) dried penne or other pasta
  shapes
sea salt and freshly ground black pepper
freshly grated Parmesan cheese, to serve

1 Cut the sausages into 2.5cm (1 inch) pieces. Heat a large sauté pan or flameproof casserole and cook the sausage pieces for 5 minutes until lightly browned.

2 Drain off the excess fat to leave just a thin coating in the pan, then add the onions and garlic. Cook for 10 minutes, stirring occasionally, until golden brown.

3 Stir in the chillies and sage and cook for 1 minute. Add the tomatoes with their juice, the sugar and some salt and pepper. Bring to the boil, then partially cover and simmer gently for 40 minutes until dark and a little pulpy.

4 Meanwhile, cook the pasta in a large pan of boiling salted water according to the packet instructions until *al dente* (tender, but firm to the bite). Drain well and return to the pan, then add the sausage sauce and toss to mix.

5 Divide the hot pasta among warm bowls. Serve with Parmesan and don't forget the pepper mill.

chorizo and cannellini bean soup

Chorizo sausage has a wonderful smoky flavour, which gives this hearty soup a real blast of Spanish sunshine. It's important to use a white-skinned potato here, as the floury texture almost dissolves into the soup to give a lovely thick finish. Serve with warm crusty bread.

SERVES 4

2 tablespoons olive oil
2 garlic cloves, peeled and chopped
1 onion, peeled and chopped
500g (1lb 2oz) floury potatoes, such as
  Maris Piper or King Edward, peeled and diced
2 teaspoons smoked paprika
1 litre (1³/4 pints) hot vegetable stock
250g (9oz) chorizo sausage, roughly diced
410g can cannellini beans, drained
sea salt and freshly ground black pepper
2 tablespoons chopped parsley, to serve

1 Heat the olive oil in a large saucepan. Add the garlic, onion and potatoes, and cook gently for about 10 minutes until golden. Stir in the paprika and stock and bring to the boil. Lower the heat and simmer for 15 minutes.

2 Stir in the chorizo sausage and cannellini beans and cook for 5 minutes or so, until piping hot. Season with a little salt and plenty of black pepper, then ladle into warm bowls and serve sprinkled with the chopped parsley.

storecupboard suppers

We all have moments when the fridge is empty and we can't face going to the supermarket, or friends call round just as you are about to start cooking supper. These are the times when we turn to the storecupboard for help. Let's face it, a well stocked cupboard is vital to keep organised on the culinary front. For suggestions of useful items to keep in stock for impromptu meals, see page 9.

If you always keep the essentials to hand, you'll be safe in the knowledge that you can keep the family fed and watered. Good starchy carbohydrates – such as rice, pasta, noodles and bread – form the basis for almost every meal, so make sure you have them in stock. With just a few flavoursome additions and a couple of fresh ingredients they can be turned into a truly satisfying supper, usually in next to no time. Here are a few quick ideas using storecupboard standbys. Each serves 2.

▲ lemony lentil and pasta soup

Cook 1 chopped onion and 1 chopped carrot in 1 tbsp olive oil with a little chopped garlic for a few minutes to soften. Stir in 400g canned tomatoes with juice, 50g (2oz) red lentils and 900ml (1½ pints) vegetable stock. Bring to the boil and simmer for 30 minutes until lentils are tender. Cook 75g (3oz) fusilli or other pasta shapes in a separate pan of boiling salted water until *al dente*. Once the lentils are cooked, stir in the drained pasta and a good squeeze of lemon juice. Season and serve.

spiced chick pea biriyani

Heat 1 tbsp sunflower oil in a flameproof casserole and cook 2 large sliced onions for 10 minutes until golden. Add ½ tsp cumin or mustard seeds and cook for 1 minute. Stir in 200g (7oz) basmati rice, 400g can chick peas, drained, 2 tbsp curry paste, 2 tbsp sultanas, 600ml (1 pint) hot vegetable stock, salt and pepper. Cover and cook in the oven at 190°C, gas 5 for 25 minutes until the rice is tender. Scatter with salted cashews.

satay noodles

Simmer 2 blocks egg noodles (about 125g) in boiling water for 3–4 minutes until tender, then drain. Heat a splash of sunflower oil in a wok and cook 1 sliced large red pepper for 2–3 minutes on a high heat. Add the noodles, a 200g carton coconut cream, 50g pack salted or dry roast peanuts, roughly chopped, a dash of soy sauce and a squeeze of lime juice. Heat, stirring, until piping hot. Divide among bowls and scatter over some coriander or sliced spring onions.

▲ cheesy bean hash

Using a fork, roughly mash 750g (1lb 10oz) boiled potatoes with 400g can baked beans and a pinch of dried chilli flakes. Heat a little sunflower oil in a large non-stick frying pan. Add the mash and cook over a low heat, without turning, for 15 minutes until the bottom is crisp and golden. Turn the hash over, roughly breaking it up, then leave to cook for another 15 minutes until the base is crisp. Stir through a handful of grated Cheddar, top with a dollop of sweet chilli sauce or ketchup and serve.

butternut chowder with cheese toasties

Choose an orange-fleshed squash, such as butternut or kabocha, for this recipe as these cook down to a wonderful velvety-textured soup. In common with many other soups, this benefits from a night in the fridge so the flavours can really develop.

SERVES 4

2 tablespoons olive oil

2 onions, peeled and finely chopped

2 garlic cloves, peeled and roughly chopped

1kg (2¼lb) peeled butternut or kabocha
  squash flesh, cubed

1 litre (1¾ pints) hot vegetable stock

4 thyme sprigs

200ml (7fl oz) crème fraîche

sea salt and freshly ground black pepper

FOR THE CHEESE TOASTIES:

40g (1½oz) easy-spread butter

8 slices of white bread

200g (7oz) Gruyère cheese, coarsely grated

20g (¾oz) chives or garlic chives, snipped

1   Heat the olive oil in a large saucepan and cook the onions, garlic and squash over a gentle heat for about 10 minutes until the onion has softened. Pour in the hot stock and stir in the thyme. Cover and simmer for 30 minutes until tender.

2   Meanwhile, butter the bread. Make up four sandwiches with the cheese and chives, keeping the butter on the outside of the sandwiches. Preheat a griddle pan or large non-stick frying pan and cook the sandwiches, two at a time, for 2–3 minutes on each side until golden brown and the cheese is molten inside. Keep hot.

3   Remove the woody thyme stalks from the soup, then purée with a hand-held blender or in a blender goblet until smooth. Return to the pan if necessary. Stir in the crème fraîche and heat through gently without boiling. Check the seasoning.

4   Cut the toasties into squares or fingers. Ladle the soup into warm bowls and serve with the toasties.

cheese and tomato macaroni

Everyone loves macaroni cheese and this is a fantastic version. It skips the hassle of making a cheese sauce and packs even more flavour with the addition of roasted sweet cherry tomatoes.

SERVES 4
250g (9oz) cherry tomatoes
1 tablespoon olive oil
350g (12oz) dried macaroni

250g tub mascarpone cheese
1 tablespoon Dijon mustard
300g (11oz) fontina cheese, coarsely grated
sea salt and freshly ground black pepper

1 Preheat the oven to 220°C (fan oven 200°C), gas mark 7. Place the cherry tomatoes in a 2 litre (3½ pint) ovenproof dish. Drizzle over the olive oil and season with salt and pepper, then roast for 15 minutes until the tomatoes have softened slightly and the skins have split.

2 Meanwhile, cook the macaroni in a large pan of boiling salted water according to the packet instructions until *al dente* (tender, but firm to the bite).

3 In a bowl, combine the mascarpone, mustard and fontina cheese, stirring until evenly blended.

4 Drain the pasta and return to the pan. Stir in the cheese mixture, then the roasted tomatoes and season with salt and pepper to taste. Tip the mixture back into the ovenproof dish used for the tomatoes. Bake for 25–30 minutes until golden brown and bubbling. Leave to stand for a few minutes, then serve straight from the dish.

roasted pepper pizzettes

If there's a better time to make these than on a lazy sunny afternoon, then I've yet to find it. The sweet, bursting cherry tomatoes and creamy soft mozzarella will have everyone coming back for more!

SERVES 6

4 x 145g packets pizza dough mix
500ml (16fl oz) warm water
flour, to dust
450g (1lb) yellow cherry tomatoes
285g jar roasted peppers in olive oil, drained
300g (11oz) mozzarella cheese, drained
2 tablespoons olive oil
sea salt and freshly ground black pepper
basil leaves, to garnish

1 Preheat the oven to 200°C (fan oven 180°C), gas mark 6. Empty the pizza dough mix into a bowl, make a well in the centre and pour in the warm water. Mix according to the packet instructions, to make a soft dough. Knead vigorously on a lightly floured surface for 5 minutes until smooth.

2 Divide the dough into six even-sized balls and roll out each roughly to a 20cm (8 inch) round. Transfer the rounds to two non-stick baking sheets and leave to rise for 10 minutes.

3 Meanwhile, halve the cherry tomatoes, cut the peppers into strips and dice the mozzarella. Arrange on top of the pizzas, drizzle over the olive oil and season with salt and pepper. Bake for 20 minutes until risen and golden brown. Tear the basil leaves over the pizzettes and serve immediately.

caramelised pepper spaghetti

Peppers are often quickly stir-fried, which leaves them wonderfully crunchy, but sometimes it's better to let gentle slow-cooking release their natural sweetness.

SERVES 6

4 tablespoons olive oil

3 red peppers, cored, deseeded and thinly sliced

3 yellow peppers, cored, deseeded and thinly sliced

1 large onion, peeled and thinly sliced

650g (1lb 7oz) dried spaghetti

2 garlic cloves, peeled and thinly sliced

1 tablespoon balsamic vinegar

20g (3/4oz) basil leaves

4 tablespoons freshly grated Parmesan cheese

sea salt and freshly ground black pepper

1 Heat the olive oil in a large sauté pan and very gently cook the peppers and onion with some salt and pepper over a low heat for 40–45 minutes, stirring from time to time, until the peppers become very soft and the onion is dark golden.

2 About 10 minutes before the peppers will be ready, cook the spaghetti in a large pan of boiling salted water according to the packet instructions until *al dente* (tender, but firm to the bite). Stir the garlic into the peppers and cook for a few more minutes. Add the vinegar and check the seasoning.

3 Drain the pasta well and return to the pan. Tear in the basil, then add the pepper mixture and Parmesan. Toss well, then serve.

garlic mushroom linguine

This easy pasta dish uses the classic pairing of garlic and mushrooms. Serve with a full-bodied Italian red wine and plenty of Parmesan.

SERVES 4

400g (14oz) dried linguine

50g (2oz) butter

2 tablespoons olive oil

3 garlic cloves, peeled and chopped

500g (1lb 2oz) chestnut mushrooms, thickly sliced

juice of 1 lemon, or to taste

20g (3/4oz) tarragon or parsley, chopped

sea salt and freshly ground black pepper

freshly grated Parmesan cheese, to serve

1 Cook the pasta in a large pan of boiling salted water according to the packet instructions until *al dente* (tender, but firm to the bite). Meanwhile, heat the butter and olive oil in a large frying pan and fry the garlic for 1 minute. Add the mushrooms with lemon juice to taste and cook for 10 minutes, stirring only once or twice, until tender and golden brown. Season generously.

2 Drain the pasta well and return to the pan. Add the mushrooms and herbs, toss well and serve, with Parmesan to pass round.

pea, mascarpone and mint risotto

This is a lovely soft risotto that's brought to the table with the mascarpone just melting. I like to serve it with chilled white wine or icy cold beers. You can make this with any type of risotto rice, but the elegant carnaroli grain is always my first choice.

SERVES 4

1 tablespoon olive oil
1 large onion, peeled and chopped
2 garlic cloves, peeled and chopped
400g (14oz) carnaroli or other risotto rice
3 rosemary sprigs
150ml (1/4 pint) Italian dry white wine
1.2 litres (2 pints) hot vegetable stock
250g (9oz) frozen garden peas
250g tub mascarpone cheese
4 tablespoons roughly chopped mint
sea salt and freshly ground black pepper
2 tablespoons freshly grated Parmesan cheese,
   to serve

1 Heat the olive oil in a large heavy-based saucepan, add the onion and garlic and cook for about 5 minutes until the onion has softened.

2 Stir in the rice and rosemary, then add the wine and cook vigorously for 2–3 minutes until it has been absorbed. Pour in half of the stock and leave to cook for 10 minutes or until the stock has been absorbed, stirring from time to time.

3 Add the rest of the stock and continue to cook for a further 5 minutes, then add the peas. Cook for another 5 minutes, stirring occasionally, until all the liquid has been absorbed and the rice is tender. Season with salt and pepper to taste, and remove the woody rosemary stalks. Ripple through the mascarpone and mint.

4 Before the mascarpone has completely melted, divide the risotto among warm bowls and top each with a sprinkle of Parmesan and a good grinding of black pepper. Serve swiftly.

3 weekends

Spanish prawn soup

This is my take on a classic bisque. The addition of paprika and paella rice give the soup an inviting Spanish flavour.

SERVES 6

750g (1lb 10oz) raw prawns (any size will do),
  thawed if frozen
large knob of butter
2 shallots, peeled and sliced
2 garlic cloves, peeled and sliced
2 ripe tomatoes, roughly chopped

1 rosemary sprig
1 tablespoon smoked paprika
pinch of dried chilli flakes
150ml (1/4 pint) dry white wine
75g (3oz) short-grain rice, such as paella
  or risotto rice
sea salt and freshly ground black pepper

1 Peel the prawns and set aside, reserving the shells. Heat the butter in a large pan and cook the shallots and garlic for 2 minutes. Add the prawn shells and cook for a further 3–4 minutes.

2 Stir in the tomatoes, rosemary, paprika and chilli flakes and cook for 1 minute. Add the wine and cook vigorously for a couple of minutes, then add 2 litres (3½ pints) water. Bring to the boil, cover and simmer gently for 20 minutes.

3 Strain the stock into a clean pan, then stir in the rice and some salt and pepper. Bring to a gentle boil and simmer for 30 minutes until the rice is very soft.

4 Add the prawns and cook for 3–5 minutes, depending on the size, until they are pink. Whiz until smooth using a hand-held blender, or whiz in a blender goblet and then reheat gently. Ladle into warm bowls and serve with warm crusty bread.

smoked haddock and prawn pie

Everyone loves fish pie. There's something about the fluffy cheesy potatoes, juicy seafood and creamy chive-speckled sauce that makes it irresistible. It's a perfect winter supper that's easier to make than you think.

SERVES 8

2kg (4½lb) floury potatoes, such as Maris Piper or King Edward, peeled and cubed
1 litre (1¾ pints) milk
750g (1lb 10oz) smoked haddock fillets
100g (3½oz) butter
75g (3oz) plain flour

100g (3½oz) Cheddar cheese, grated
300ml (½ pint) soured cream
150g (5oz) frozen peas, thawed
400g (14oz) peeled raw tiger prawns, thawed if frozen
20g (¾oz) chives, snipped
sea salt and freshly ground black pepper

1 Cook the potatoes in a large pan of boiling salted water for 15–20 minutes until tender.

2 Meanwhile, pour the milk into a sauté pan and add the smoked haddock. Bring gently to the boil, then remove from the heat and leave to stand for 5 minutes. Using a slotted spoon, transfer the smoked haddock to a plate and set aside. Measure out 200ml (7fl oz) of the milk for the mash; the rest will be used in the sauce.

3 To make the sauce, melt 75g (3oz) of the butter in a heavy-based pan. Stir in the flour and cook for 1 minute. Gradually whisk in the milk for the sauce. Bring to the boil, stirring, then simmer gently for 3–4 minutes.

4 Preheat the oven to 200°C (fan oven 180°C), gas mark 6. Drain the potatoes and mash well. Stir in the milk reserved for the mash, the remaining butter, the cheese and some seasoning.

5 Stir the soured cream and peas into the sauce together with the prawns and heat gently for a couple of minutes without boiling. Pour into a deep ovenproof dish. Stir in the chives. Flake in the haddock, discarding any skin, and season to taste.

6 Spoon the mash over the top to cover the filling and rough up the surface, using a fork. Place the dish on a baking sheet and bake for 30 minutes until bubbling around the edges and golden brown.

olive oil-poached salmon with linguine and lemon

This is very simple, but quite an elegant dish. Slowly cooking the salmon in olive oil gives it a lovely flavour and keeps it perfectly moist.

SERVES 6

800g (1³/₄lb) salmon fillet, cut into
  6 even-sized pieces
1 lemon, peeled and thinly sliced
2 tablespoons roughly chopped tarragon
1 teaspoon black peppercorns, roughly crushed
1 teaspoon fine sea salt
200ml (7fl oz) olive oil
600g (1¹/₄lb) dried linguine
75g (3oz) sun-blushed tomatoes, finely chopped
100g (3¹/₂oz) wild rocket

1 Preheat the oven to 150°C (fan oven 130°C), gas mark 2. Arrange the pieces of salmon in a shallow baking tin and place the lemon slices on top. Scatter over the tarragon, peppercorns and salt, and pour over the olive oil. Bake for 30 minutes until the salmon is cooked.

2 Meanwhile, cook the pasta in a large pan of boiling salted water according to the packet instructions until *al dente* (tender, but firm to the bite). Drain and return to the pan.

3 Lift the salmon out of the oil and break it into large flakes, directly into the pan of pasta. Add 1–2 tablespoons of the olive oil together with the lemon slices, sun-blushed tomatoes and rocket, and toss together gently. Divide among warm bowls and serve.

silky chicken noodle soup

My friend, chef Ben O'Donoghue, from the television series 'The Best', showed me how to cook chicken this way – the bird is steeped in a fragrant stock rather than poached. This is a traditional Chinese method and gives the chicken a lovely tender texture.

SERVES 8

1 large chicken, about 2kg (4½lb), cut
   into 8 pieces
1 red onion, peeled and roughly chopped
6 garlic cloves, peeled and thickly sliced
4cm (1½ inch) piece of fresh root ginger,
   peeled and thickly sliced
2 lemon grass stalks, lightly flattened
   with a rolling pin
2 red chillies, thickly sliced

8 kaffir lime leaves, fresh or dried
1 teaspoon fine sea salt
200g (7oz) fine egg noodles
250g (9oz) pak choi, sliced
125g (4oz) shiitake mushrooms, sliced
3 tablespoons soy sauce
1 tablespoon wine vinegar
200g (7oz) bean sprouts
handful of coriander leaves
1 teaspoon toasted sesame oil

1 Remove the skin from the chicken pieces, then place them in a very large pan. Add the onion, garlic, ginger, lemon grass, chillies, lime leaves and salt. Cover with water – you will need about 3 litres (5 pints). Bring to the boil, skimming off any surface residue. Cover with a lid, remove from the heat and leave to cool. The chicken will cook in the residual heat (once cooled, it can be chilled overnight).

2 Strain the stock into a clean pan. Lift out the chicken from the sieve and discard the flavourings. Using your fingers, tear the chicken meat from the bones and set aside. Gently reheat the stock.

3 Meanwhile, cook the egg noodles in a separate pan of boiling water according to the packet instructions. Drain the noodles and divide among eight warm bowls.

4 Stir the shredded chicken, pak choi and mushrooms into the hot stock and cook for 1 minute. Add the soy sauce and vinegar.

5 Pile the bean sprouts on top of the noodles, then ladle over the chicken and vegetable broth. Scatter over some coriander leaves and add a drop or two of sesame oil to each bowl. Serve at once.

Peking duck noodles

Peking duck does take a bit of preparation time, but my version is much simpler than the classic Chinese method and well worth the effort. It makes an impressive dinner party dish too.

SERVES 6

1 plump duck, about 2kg (4½lb)
1 tablespoon dark muscovado sugar
2 teaspoons sea salt
3 x 150g packets vacuum-packed
   straight-to-wok noodles
1 tablespoon sunflower oil
4cm (1½ inch) piece root ginger, peeled and diced

1 vegetable stock cube
1 tablespoon cornflour, mixed with a little water
2 tablespoons sweet chilli sauce
1 tablespoon soy sauce
4 Chinese leaves, shredded
1 red chilli, deseeded and finely chopped
4 spring onions, thinly sliced
small handful of basil leaves, to serve

1 Pierce the duck in several places with a skewer. Place on a rack over a roasting tin and pour over a kettle of boiling water. Drain off the water and pat the duck dry with kitchen paper, then put back on the rack. Mix the sugar and salt and rub into the duck skin. Leave in a cool, dry place for 2 hours.

2 Preheat the oven to 200°C (fan oven 180°C), gas mark 6. Pat the duck dry again, then roast for 1½ hours, basting from time to time, until the skin is crisp and dark and the meat is cooked through – pierce the thigh to check that it's not at all pink. Leave to rest for 10 minutes.

3 Meanwhile, put the noodles in a bowl, cover with boiling water and leave for 2–3 minutes, then drain. Heat a wok, add the oil and, when hot, add the noodles and ginger. Cook for 3 minutes without stirring so the noodles on the base crisp. Dissolve the stock cube in 300ml (½ pint) boiling water.

4 Stir to break up the noodles. Add the stock, cornflour, chilli and soy sauces, Chinese leaves, chilli and spring onions and stir-fry for 2–3 minutes. Using a cleaver or strong knife, cut the duck into pieces. Divide the noodle mixture among warm plates and top with the duck. Serve scattered with basil leaves.

chunky chicken and potato pie

A wonderful pie, with a delicious creamy flavour. It freezes very well, but make sure you allow plenty of time for it to thaw in the fridge.

SERVES 6

1 tablespoon olive oil

9 large skinless chicken thigh fillets, trimmed and quartered

2 potatoes, peeled and cut into 2cm (3/4 inch) dice

1 red onion, peeled and cut into wedges

2 medium leeks, trimmed and thickly sliced

3 garlic cloves, peeled and halved

1 bay leaf

1 tablespoon plain flour

50g (2oz) frozen peas

150ml (1/4 pint) crème fraîche

150ml (1/4 pint) chicken stock

small bunch of flat leaf parsley, roughly chopped

375g packet puff pastry, thawed if frozen

1 egg, beaten, to glaze

sea salt and freshly ground black pepper

1 Preheat the oven to 190°C (fan oven 170°C), gas mark 5. Put the olive oil in a small roasting tin or a large pie dish and add the chicken, potatoes, red onion, leeks, garlic cloves, bay leaf and flour. Toss well together, then season with salt and pepper. Roast for 25–30 minutes until tender, turning the chicken and vegetables occasionally.

2 Add the frozen peas, then stir in the crème fraîche, chicken stock and parsley. If you have time, leave the filling to cool.

3 Roll out the pastry until 2.5cm (1 inch) larger all round than the size of the roasting tin or pie dish. Lay the pastry over the filling, tucking in the edges down the sides of the tin, or pressing them on to the rim of pie dish (first brushing the rim with a little water).

4 Brush the top of the pie with beaten egg to glaze, then bake for 25–30 minutes until the pastry is risen and golden. Serve hot.

lemon chicken with sweet potato and rosemary mash

Preserved lemons lend a delicious Middle Eastern flavour to roast chicken, and soft, creamy roast sweet potato purée is a fabulous accompaniment.

SERVES 6

2 free-range chickens, each about 1.5kg
  (3¼lb), each cut into 8 pieces
12 garlic cloves
8 thyme sprigs
8 small preserved or pickled lemons, halved
25g (1oz) butter
sea salt and freshly ground black pepper

FOR THE MASH:
2kg (4½lb) sweet potatoes, peeled and
  thickly sliced
1 tablespoon olive oil
1 tablespoon chopped rosemary
5–6 tablespoons crème fraîche

1 Preheat the oven to 200°C (fan oven 180°C), gas mark 6. Pack the chicken pieces, garlic, thyme and lemons snugly in a large roasting tin. Season generously with salt and pepper, then dot over the butter. Roast for 40 minutes until golden brown and cooked through.

2 Meanwhile, put the sweet potato slices in another roasting tin and stir in the olive oil, rosemary and some salt and pepper. Roast for 30 minutes until tender and golden. Roughly mash the sweet potatoes in the tin, then stir in the crème fraîche using a wooden spoon.

3 Divide the chicken among warm plates, making sure everyone gets some garlic and preserved lemon. Serve the sweet potato mash on the side.

lamb and red cabbage hotpot

Here is the perfect comfort food to warm up a cold winter evening. This hearty dinner takes a while to cook but it's very easy to prepare. I've used a boned shoulder of lamb, but you could use neck fillet or boned leg if you prefer.
Illustrated on previous page

SERVES 6

2–3 tablespoons vegetable oil
1.5kg (3¼lb) boneless shoulder of lamb,
    trimmed of excess fat and cut into large cubes
2 tablespoons plain flour
1 large onion, peeled and sliced
4 garlic cloves, peeled and thinly sliced
6 thyme sprigs
1 small red cabbage, about 500g (1lb 2oz),
    cored and thinly sliced
150ml (¼ pint) ruby port
750ml (1¼ pints) lamb stock
4 teaspoons balsamic vinegar
1kg (2¼lb) red skinned potatoes, such as Desirée
25g (1oz) butter, melted
sea salt and freshly ground black pepper

1   Heat the oil in a large flameproof casserole. Dust the lamb with the flour and fry in batches for 3–4 minutes, stirring, until nicely browned all over.

2   Once all the meat is browned and set aside on a plate, add the onion to the pan and cook for 5–8 minutes until soft and golden. Add the garlic and thyme and cook for a further minute or so.

3   Return the lamb to the pan, along with any juices on the plate. Stir in the cabbage, port, stock and vinegar. Bring to the boil, cover and simmer gently for 1–1½ hours until the lamb is very tender.

4   Meanwhile, preheat the oven to 200°C (fan oven 180°C), gas mark 6. Cook the potatoes in boiling salted water for 15 minutes. Drain and thickly slice.

5   Uncover the casserole and arrange the sliced potatoes over the lamb and and cabbage. Brush the potatoes with the melted butter and bake, uncovered, for 30 minutes until they are golden brown. Serve straight from the casserole.

slow-roast leg of lamb in wine

Slow-cooking a whole leg of lamb in wine ensures it turns out meltingly tender and juicy. Rosemary, the classic herb for lamb, adds flavour and fragrance and is balanced by a touch of sweetness from redcurrant jelly.

SERVES 6

2 tablespoons olive oil
1 leg of lamb, about 2kg (4¹/₂lb)
2 tablespoons plain flour
2 onions, peeled and thinly sliced
4 rosemary sprigs
4 garlic cloves, peeled and thinly sliced
2 x 75cl bottles dry white wine, or 1 bottle
  plus 750ml (1¹/₄ pints) lamb stock
2 tablespoons redcurrant jelly
sea salt and freshly ground black pepper

1   Preheat the oven to 170°C (fan oven 150°C), gas mark 3. Pour the olive oil into a large, sturdy roasting tin and set it on the hob to heat. Season the lamb, then roll it in the flour. Brown the lamb all over in the hot oil for 5–10 minutes.

2   Add the onions and cook for a further 5–10 minutes, turning the lamb and stirring the onions, until both are nicely browned. Add the rosemary, garlic, white wine (and stock if using) and redcurrant jelly. Bring to a simmer.

3   Transfer to the oven and cook for 3–3¹/₂ hours, basting the lamb now and again with the liquor. There should be a good quantity of liquor left in the bottom of the tin to serve with the lamb; if you feel it is getting too dry, just cover with foil.

4   Take the lamb out of the tin, place on a large warm platter and set aside to rest in a warm place. Meanwhile, put the tin back on the hob and simmer the pan juices for a few minutes, reducing the liquid if there is a lot, to make a tasty gravy.

5   Cut the lamb into thick slices – you'll find the meat falls away from the bone so you may end up with more chunks than slices. Serve with creamy mashed potatoes and the wine gravy.

meatball curry with coriander breads and raita

This saucy dish isn't overly hot, so the cooling raita is not strictly necessary, but it does go well. Be sure you have plenty of chapattis on hand to scoop up all the lovely, spicy sauce.

SERVES 6

3 garlic cloves, peeled and quartered
2 red chillies, roughly chopped
1 thick slice of white bread, about 50g (2oz)
1 teaspoon cumin seeds
4 tablespoons mint leaves
750g (1lb 10oz) lean lamb mince
1 egg, beaten
1–2 tablespoons vegetable oil
2 large onions, peeled and sliced
4 tomatoes, roughly chopped
500ml (16fl oz) hot lamb stock
3 tablespoons hot curry paste
sea salt and freshly ground black pepper

FOR THE RAITA:
200g (7oz) Greek yogurt
1 small cucumber, peeled and roughly chopped
2 tablespoons chopped mint
1 garlic clove, peeled and crushed
pinch of caster sugar
pinch of fine sea salt
squeeze of lemon juice

TO SERVE:
12 chapattis
25g (1oz) butter, melted
2 teaspoons ground coriander
small handful of mint leaves
1 lemon, cut into wedges

1 Put the garlic into a food processor with the chillies and tear in the bread. Add the cumin seeds and mint and pulse until finely chopped. Transfer to a bowl and stir in the minced lamb, beaten egg and plenty of salt and pepper. With damp hands, shape the mixture into walnut-sized balls.

2 Heat a splash of oil in a large non-stick sauté pan and fry the meatballs in batches over a high heat for 3–4 minutes until nicely browned. Once all the meatballs are browned and set aside, add the onions to the pan and cook for 5–8 minutes until softened and golden. Add the tomatoes and cook for a further 2–3 minutes until they become a little pulpy.

3 Return the meatballs to the pan together with the lamb stock and curry paste. Stir gently to mix. Bring to the boil and simmer gently for 30 minutes.

4 For the raita, combine the yogurt, cucumber, mint and garlic in a bowl, then stir in the sugar, salt and lemon juice to taste. Keep chilled.

5 When ready to serve, preheat a griddle pan. Brush each chapatti with a little melted butter, sprinkle with ground coriander and cook on the hot griddle pan for 1 minute until speckled with brown. Divide the curry between warm bowls and scatter with mint leaves. Serve with the raita, chapattis and lemon wedges.

thick-crust beef and stout pie

This is a wonderful old-school steak pie with a delicious full flavour and a thick, firm pastry crust – arguably the best bit. Serve with mashed potatoes and English mustard.

SERVES 8

2 tablespoons olive oil

knob of butter

2 large onions, peeled and sliced

4 garlic cloves, peeled and chopped

4 tablespoons plain flour

1.5kg (3¼lb) stewing or braising steak, cubed

2 x 500ml bottles chocolate stout or brown ale

3 tablespoons soft brown sugar

2 thyme sprigs

sea salt and freshly ground black pepper

FOR THE CRUST:

75g (3oz) lard, diced

250g (9oz) plain flour

¼ teaspoon fine sea salt

1 egg, beaten, to glaze

  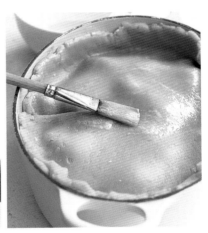

1 Heat the olive oil and butter in a flameproof casserole and cook the onions and garlic for 5 minutes until softened. Meanwhile, season the flour with salt and pepper and use to dust the steak.

2 Using a slotted spoon, lift out the onions and reserve. Brown the steak in the casserole in two batches. Return all the meat and the onions to the pan. Pour in the chocolate stout, then stir in the sugar, thyme and seasoning. Bring to the boil, partially cover and simmer very gently for 2 hours.

3 Preheat the oven to 200°C (fan oven 180°C), gas mark 6. To make the crust, heat the lard with 100ml (3½fl oz) water in a non-stick pan. Once boiling, shoot in the flour and salt, and stir with a wooden spoon until you have a smooth dough that forms a ball. Leave to cool for a few minutes.

4 Roll the dough out to a rough circle and use to cover the casserole. Brush the crust with the beaten egg and make a small hole in the middle so that steam can escape. Stand the casserole on a baking sheet. Bake for 30 minutes, then lower the oven temperature to 170°C (fan oven 150°C), gas mark 3 and bake for a further 1 hour until deep golden.

boiled ham in fragrant broth with sticky rice

An unusual twist on boiled ham, this is really fantastic. It is served with sticky rice and a ladleful of stock, although traditionalists can have their ham with mash if preferred.

SERVES 8

1 unsmoked prime gammon joint,
  about 2.2kg (4³/₄lb)
10cm (4 inch) piece fresh root ginger,
  roughly chopped
2 garlic cloves, peeled and roughly chopped
2 tomatoes, roughly chopped
1 bunch of spring onions
2 star anise
400g (14oz) sushi rice

1 Put the ham into a large pan with the ginger, garlic and tomatoes. Cut off and reserve the green part of the spring onions for serving. Slice the white part of the onions and add to the pan with the star anise. Cover with 3 litres (5 pints) cold water.

2 Bring to the boil, then partially cover the pan and simmer very gently for 3 hours, skimming the surface frequently. Towards the end of the time, cook the rice according to the packet instructions.

3 Carefully lift the ham on to a board, reserving the liquor, and leave to rest for a couple of minutes. In the meantime, finely slice the green spring onion. Carve the ham into slices.

4 Divide the rice among eight warm shallow bowls or soup plates and place the ham slices alongside. Strain the reserved liquor, then ladle some into each bowl and scatter with the spring onion (adding the star anise to a couple of bowls if you like). Serve swiftly.

salt and pepper spare ribs

For the popular oriental restaurant version of this dish, the spare ribs are typically deep-fried, but I prefer to roast them. Serve with noodles or a simple salad.

SERVES 4

2 tablespoons plain flour
1 tablespoon Chinese five spice powder
1/2 teaspoon fine sea salt
1/2 teaspoon crushed black pepper
1kg (2 1/4 lb) pork spare ribs
1 tablespoon sunflower oil
1 bunch of spring onions, trimmed and
  thinly sliced
1 red chilli, deseeded and thinly sliced
1 garlic clove, peeled and finely chopped
2 tablespoons soy sauce

1 Preheat the oven to 200°C (fan oven 180°C), gas mark 6. In a large bowl, mix together the flour, five spice powder, salt and pepper. Roll each rib in the seasoned flour, then place side by side on a rack over a roasting tin.

2 Roast for 40–50 minutes, turning from time to time, until cooked through and beautifully browned. Arrange the ribs on a large platter.

3 Heat a wok, then add the oil. When it is hot, add the spring onions and chilli and stir-fry over a high heat for 1 minute. Add the garlic and cook for a further 1 minute. Tip the contents of the wok over the ribs, then drizzle with the soy sauce. Serve immediately.

effortless entertaining

When it comes to dinner parties, I have five key points of advice to offer: plan in advance, keep it simple, prepare ahead, cut corners and wash up as you go along. Stick to things you've cooked before or recipes that look easy. Once you've decided what you're going to cook, write a detailed shopping list, checking that you haven't missed anything.

Do as much as you can ahead of time. Choose a dessert than can be prepared the day before. Either make a cold pudding that sits overnight in the fridge or freezer, like Bellini jellies (page 170), or frozen berry yogurt and meringue pots (illustrated right), or a pudding that goes in the oven as you sit down to the main course, such as oaty ginger pear crumble (page 189). Then once your guests have arrived all you need to concentrate on is the main course.

Similarly opt for an easy starter, such as one of the following ideas; each serves 6.

▲ **Italian antipasti**
Arrange 200g (7oz) sliced cured meats, such as Milano salami, bresaola and Parma ham, on a serving platter. Drizzle with a little olive oil, shave over some Parmesan and finish with a good grinding of black pepper. On a board, place a large wedge of Dolcelatte, a glass full of breadsticks and a bowl of mixed olives with some cocktail sticks. Pass round some rosemary and garlic focaccia.

chilled fire soup shots

Put a peeled, roughly chopped cucumber into a food processor with 1kg (2¼lb) roughly chopped tomatoes, 2 chopped red chillies, juice of 1 lime and some salt. Whiz until well blended and slushy. Pour into a muslin-lined large sieve set over a bowl and leave to drip for several hours – don't force through or it will turn cloudy. Chill until required. Stir in a little finely chopped coriander and serve in shot glasses.

salmon pâté

Flake a 125g packet roasted salmon into a bowl and mix in 200g (7oz) soft cheese, ½ tsp creamed horseradish, some chopped chives and a squeeze of lemon juice. Add salt and pepper to taste. Serve with triangles of warm toast.

▲ frozen berry yogurt pots

Prepare-ahead desserts are the key to easy entertaining. For this simple fruity ice, frozen summer berries and crumbled meringues are folded through creamy yogurt (see recipe, page 169). Make well in advance and freeze in freezerproof serving dishes, so you can serve them from the freezer.

▲ pan-fried haloumi with fennel salad

Using a swivel peeler, shave 2 small fennel bulbs into wafer-thin slices, put into a bowl of chilled water and refrigerate for an hour to curl and crisp. For the dressing, whisk the juice of 1 orange with 4 tbsp olive oil, seasoning and 2 tbsp chopped mint or tarragon. Cut 250g (9oz) haloumi into 6 slices, dust with seasoned flour and fry in olive oil for 2 minutes on each side until golden. Drain the fennel and pile on to plates. Top with the haloumi, pour over the dressing and serve swiftly.

aubergine, feta and broad bean salad

This amazing salad is packed with Greek-style flavours and always makes me think of the sun. The avocado oil imparts a wonderful flavour, but you can substitute olive oil if you prefer. Serve with warm pitta breads and a bowl of salad leaves as a summery lunch or supper.

SERVES 6

3 tablespoons olive oil
4 large aubergines, cut into cubes
150g (5oz) podded fresh or frozen broad beans
1 large red onion, peeled and thinly sliced
juice of 1 lemon
3 tablespoons avocado oil

250g (9oz) baby plum tomatoes, halved
1 garlic clove, peeled and crushed
2 tablespoons finely chopped pitted black olives
2 tablespoons finely chopped mint
2 x 200g (7oz) feta cheese, roughly crumbled
sea salt and freshly ground black pepper

1 Preheat the oven to 220°C (fan oven 200°C), gas mark 7. Pour the olive oil into a shallow roasting tin and place in the oven to heat. Add the aubergine cubes, toss to coat in the hot oil and roast for 30 minutes, turning from time to time, until cooked through and golden brown.

2 Meanwhile, add the broad beans to a pan of boiling water, bring back to the boil and simmer for 2 minutes or until tender. Drain well. If you have time, once the beans are cool enough to handle, pop them out of their skins. This is quite time-consuming, but worth the effort as the skins can be tough.

3 Tip the broad beans into a large bowl and add the red onion, lemon juice, 2 tablespoons of the avocado oil and the tomatoes.

4 In another bowl, stir together the garlic, olives, mint and remaining avocado oil. Lightly fold in the crumbled feta and set aside.

5 Once the aubergine is cooked, tip it into the bowl of tomatoes and broad beans, and mix well. Season with salt and pepper to taste, then set aside for 5 minutes, or leave to cool to room temperature. Divide among serving plates and spoon over the feta mixture to serve.

Taleggio and thyme risotto

Risotto is a brilliant any-occasion dish. The addition of some soft, flavoursome Taleggio and fresh thyme makes this one rather special.

SERVES 6

50g (2oz) butter
1 red onion, peeled and finely chopped
2 garlic cloves, peeled and finely chopped
1 teaspoon thyme leaves
500g packet carnaroli risotto rice
300ml (½ pint) Italian dry white wine

1.2 litres (2 pints) hot vegetable stock
2 x 250g packets Taleggio cheese,
  roughly chopped
4 tablespoons chopped parsley
sea salt and freshly ground black pepper
4 tablespoons freshly grated Parmesan
  cheese, to serve

1   Heat the butter in a large pan and cook the onion with the garlic and thyme leaves for 5 minutes until softened and golden. Add the rice and stir to coat with the butter.

2   Pour in the wine and bubble vigorously for 5 minutes or so until the liquid has been absorbed. Gradually add the stock, roughly one-quarter at a time, stirring and simmering until each batch has been absorbed before adding the next. Total cooking time will be about 20 minutes.

3   Remove the risotto from the heat and stir through the Taleggio and parsley. Check the seasoning, adding salt and pepper to taste. Divide among warm serving bowls and top each with a sprinkling of freshly grated Parmesan.

red pepper and fontina cous cous cake

This makes a lovely light lunch, perfect with a rocket and tomato salad and some chilled red wine. In order to make the cous cous hold together, it needs to be slightly over-moistened, which is why there is more stock than usual.

SERVES 4

300g (11oz) cous cous
450ml (3/4 pint) hot vegetable stock
juice of 1 lime
2 tablespoons olive oil
1/2 x 280g jar roasted red peppers, drained and
    cut into 1cm (1/2 inch) wide strips
200g (7oz) fontina or Gruyère cheese,
    cut into small dice
1 egg, beaten
4 tablespoons snipped chives
freshly ground black pepper

1 Put the cous cous into a large heatproof bowl. Stir together the vegetable stock, lime juice and a good grinding of black pepper, then pour over the cous cous. Leave for 15 minutes until all the stock has been absorbed.

2 Heat a splash of the olive oil in a 23cm (9 inch) non-stick frying pan. Stir the peppers, cheese, egg and chives into the cous cous, then tip into the pan and pat down well into a cake. Cook over a gentle heat for 15 minutes, without touching, until the base is crisp and golden.

3 Carefully slide the cous cous cake on to a plate, then invert back into the pan, adding the rest of the oil if needed. Cook for a further 10 minutes or so until the other side is golden. Slide back on to the plate and cut into wedges to serve.

cheese and onion baked potatoes

These are the most delicious jacket potatoes I have ever eaten. Simple, but sumptuously tasty. I keep the red onions raw, because I like the freshness they offer, but you can soften them first in a little olive oil if you prefer.

SERVES 6

6 baking potatoes, each about 250g (9oz)
1 tablespoon olive oil
coarse sea salt, to sprinkle
2 small red onions, peeled and very
  finely chopped
75g (3oz) Gruyère or Emmental cheese, grated
75g (3oz) mature Cheddar cheese, grated
300ml (1/2 pint) soured cream
sea salt and freshly ground black pepper

1 Preheat the oven to 200°C (fan oven 180°C), gas mark 6. Pierce the potatoes in several places with a fork, then rub with the olive oil and sprinkle with salt. Bake directly on the middle oven shelf for 1 hour and 20 minutes, turning from time to time.

2 To check that the potatoes are cooked, wrap them in a clean tea towel and give them a gentle squeeze – they should feel soft. Keeping each potato wrapped in the tea towel, hit each one with your fist, so that the skin splits (this looks more natural than cutting them open).

3 Scoop the fluffy flesh out of the potatoes and place in a bowl. Stir in the onions, grated cheeses, soured cream and some salt and pepper. Roughly pile back into the potato shells. Place on a baking sheet and bake for 30–40 minutes until golden brown. Serve hot, with salad or baked beans.

4 lunchboxes and snacks

sticky lemon chicken wings

Easy and delicious, baked chicken wings are the ideal late-night snack, eaten hot from the oven. Or you can eat them cold the next day, packed in a lunchbox or picnic basket.

SERVES 4

12 large chicken wings
25g (1oz) butter, melted
grated zest and juice of 1 lemon
1 teaspoon chilli powder
1/4 teaspoon sea salt

1 Preheat the oven to 200°C (fan oven 180°C), gas mark 6. Using a strong pair of scissors, snip the tip off each wing and discard.

2 Mix together the melted butter, lemon zest and juice, chilli powder and salt.

3 Arrange the chicken wings on a rack set over a baking tray and brush both sides with the lemony butter. Roast for 30–40 minutes, turning and basting once or twice, until golden brown.

Parma ham and mozzarella focaccia

Here a classic focaccia dough is reinforced with potato to give a gorgeous texture that really satisfies. Cut into wedges and eat in place of a regular sandwich.

SERVES 6

250g (9oz) floury potatoes, such as Maris Piper or King Edward, peeled and cubed
1kg (2¼lb) Italian '00' white bread flour
7g sachet fast-action dried yeast
2 x 85g packets sliced Parma ham, roughly torn
300g (11oz) mozzarella cheese, drained and diced

6 sun-dried tomatoes in oil, drained and diced
1 teaspoon fine salt
2 tablespoons olive oil
2 tablespoons Italian or French chilli oil (not oriental style)
1 teaspoon coarse sea salt
1 rosemary sprig, roughly chopped

1 Cook the potatoes in a large pan of boiling salted water for 15 minutes until tender. Drain well and turn into a large bowl. Mash thoroughly, then leave to cool.

2 Tip the mash on to a lightly floured surface and add the flour, yeast, ham, mozzarella, sun-dried tomatoes and fine salt. Make a well in the centre and add the olive oil and 400ml (14fl oz) warm water. Gradually incorporate the dry ingredients into the liquid and mix to a soft dough, adding a little warm water if needed.

3 Knead the dough on a floured surface for a good 5 minutes until smooth. Roll out to a large oval shape, about 1cm (½ inch) thick. Transfer to a baking sheet, cover with a clean tea towel and leave to rise for an hour or so until doubled in size.

4 Preheat the oven to 200°C (fan oven 180°C), gas mark 6. Using your fingertips, make indentations about 2cm (¾ inch) deep all over the surface of the dough. Drizzle with the chilli oil and sprinkle with sea salt and rosemary. Bake for 35–40 minutes until risen and golden brown. Allow to cool for a few minutes before slicing.

chicken palm pies

These lovely little pies are so named because they fit neatly in the palm of your hand. They are perfect for lunchboxes, and ideal for freezing.
Illustrated on previous page

MAKES 12

75g (3oz) cubed pancetta, or dry-cured streaky bacon, cut into small strips
4 large skinless chicken thigh fillets
1 teaspoon cornflour
1 small onion, peeled and finely chopped
1 teaspoon chopped sage
100ml (3½fl oz) chicken stock
squeeze of lemon juice
500g (1lb 2oz) ready-made shortcrust pastry
1 egg yolk
sea salt and freshly ground black pepper

1 Cook the pancetta or bacon in a large non-stick frying pan for 3–4 minutes until crisp and golden brown. Remove with a slotted spoon and set aside.

2 Cut the chicken thighs into 1cm (½ inch) pieces and dust with the cornflour. Add to the frying pan with the onion and cook for 8–10 minutes until well browned and cooked through, adding the sage for the last minute of the cooking time.

3 Stir in the stock and bring to the boil. Season with salt and pepper and add a squeeze of lemon juice to taste, then leave to cool.

4 Preheat the oven to 200°C (fan oven 180°C), gas mark 6. Roll out three-quarters of the pastry, stamp out twelve 15cm (6 inch) discs and use to line a 12-hole muffin tin, allowing excess pastry to overhang the edges. Roll out the remaining pastry and stamp out twelve 7.5cm (3 inch) discs for lids.

5 Stir the pancetta or bacon into the chicken mixture, then divide among the pastry cases. Dampen the inside edges of the pastry cases with a little water. Lay the pastry lids on top of the filling, then fold the edges of the pastry case over and press together to seal. Cut a small hole in the top of each pie.

6 Mix together the egg yolk and ¼ teaspoon salt. Brush over the pies, then bake for 20 minutes until the pastry is crisp and well glazed. Leave to cool. Wrap individually in waxed or greaseproof paper to pack into lunchboxes.

sesame chicken noodle salad

This oriental-style salad is a tasty, satisfying alternative to lunchbox sandwiches. Either buy cooked chicken portions from the deli counter, or use chicken leftover from the Sunday roast.

SERVES 2

75g (3oz) flat rice noodles
175g (6oz) cooked chicken breast
1 tablespoon soy sauce
2 tablespoons sweet chilli sauce
4 spring onions, trimmed and finely chopped
2 teaspoons sesame seeds, toasted
½ teaspoon toasted sesame oil
handful of coriander leaves, roughly torn
sea salt and freshly ground black pepper

1 Put the rice noodles into a heatproof bowl. Pour on boiling water to cover generously and leave to soak for 5 minutes.

2 Meanwhile, remove the skin from the chicken breast and cut the flesh into fine strips. Place in a bowl, add the soy sauce and chilli sauce, and toss to mix.

3 Drain the rice noodles, refresh under cold running water and drain thoroughly. Add to the chicken strips with the spring onions, sesame seeds and sesame oil. Toss well and season with salt and pepper to taste. Add the coriander leaves.

4 Either serve at once or pack into plastic tubs for lunchboxes.

wraps and sandwiches

With the fantastic selection of breads now readily available – and a little imagination – the humble sandwich can be turned into a delicious and satisfying meal. I've become a real fan of the flat bread and there are plenty to choose from, including flour tortillas, pitta breads, naans, chapattis and Californian wraps.

All flat breads become a little softer and easier to roll if you heat them very briefly, either in a dry frying pan or for a few seconds in a microwave. Once filled and rolled, wrap in greaseproof paper, twisting the ends to secure. When ready to eat, peel down the paper like a banana skin.

There's no limit to the variety of fillings. Try grilled aubergine slices with feta and tzatziki, Parma ham and Taleggio with torn basil, sliced beef with peppery rocket and horseradish, or cold roast pork (page 160) with a little redcurrant jelly – my favourite. Or try one of the following original ideas.

▲ **spicy omelette chapatti**
To make 1, heat 1 tsp oil in a small frying pan, add 1 chopped green chilli, 1 chopped spring onion and 3 halved cherry tomatoes and cook for 2–3 minutes. Stir in 1 tsp garam masala and cook for 1 minute. Swirl in 1 lightly beaten large egg and cook until the base is set. Flip the omelette over and cook for a minute on the other side. Place the omelette on top of a chapatti and spoon over 1 tbsp sweet chilli sauce. Roll up and wrap in greaseproof paper, then foil.

chicken tikka wraps

To serve 4, cut 4 small skinless chicken breast fillets into 1cm (1/2 inch) strips. Coat in 150g (5oz) yogurt mixed with 1 crushed garlic clove, 1 tsp ground cumin, 1/4 tsp cayenne, 1/4 tsp ground turmeric and 1/2 tsp salt. Grill on a foil-lined tray, turning until cooked through. Divide between 4 warm flour tortilla wraps, scatter with shredded iceberg lettuce and roll up tightly, then wrap in greaseproof paper. Serve with lemon wedges.

skewered lamb and aubergine pittas

To serve 2, combine 1/4 chopped cucumber, 2 roughly chopped tomatoes and a handful of chopped mint in a bowl. Squeeze over a little lemon juice, add a drizzle of olive oil and season well. Toast 2 pitta breads in the toaster or under the grill. Split open and spoon 2 tbsp ready-made aubergine dip into each. Slide the meat from 2 ready-cooked lamb skewers (from the deli counter) into each pitta and spoon over the tomato and cucumber salad. Wrap in foil.

▲ crusty Tex-Mex roll

To make 1, slice the top 1–2cm (1/2– 3/4 inch) off a crusty roll and remove most of the bread from the inside, leaving a layer, about 1cm (1/2 inch) thick, inside the crust. Fill with a few spoonfuls of canned refried beans, 1/2 finely chopped green chilli, a handful of grated Cheddar cheese and a dollop of soured cream. Replace the top of the roll and wrap in cling film or waxed paper. Leave for an hour before eating.

potato pasties

A whole box of filo pastry makes a lot of pasties, which is terrific as they freeze brilliantly – simply pack them in pairs in small bags. Once thawed you can warm them up in the oven.

MAKES 10

750g (1lb 10oz) floury potatoes, such as Maris Piper or King Edward, peeled and cubed
1 tablespoon olive oil
2 shallots, peeled and finely chopped
1 garlic clove, peeled and finely chopped
1 teaspoon cayenne pepper
1 teaspoon made English mustard
200g (7oz) Cheddar cheese, coarsely grated
200g (7oz) ready-made filo pastry (10 sheets)
25g (1oz) butter, melted
sea salt and freshly ground black pepper

1   Cook the potatoes in a pan of boiling salted water for 15 minutes until tender.

2   Meanwhile, heat the olive oil in a large non-stick frying pan and gently cook the shallots and garlic for 2–3 minutes. Drain the potatoes well and add to the frying pan, mashing them roughly with a fork. Leave to cool.

3   Preheat the oven to 200°C (fan oven 180°C), gas mark 6. Stir the cayenne, mustard and cheese into the potato mixture, seasoning generously with salt and pepper.

4   Cut each sheet of filo pastry in half lengthways to give twenty 30 x 9cm (12 x 3½ inch) strips. Place two strips of pastry on a surface, overlapping them at right angles to form an L shape. Spoon some of the potato mixture on to the overlapped corner, then fold over the two strips alternately to enclose the filling. Turn over, then fold the two strips back over so that you make a square parcel with all four sides enclosed.

5   Brush lightly with melted butter and transfer to a non-stick baking sheet. Bake for 20 minutes until crisp and golden brown. Serve warm, or cool on a wire rack before wrapping in greaseproof paper or foil.

butternut squash and Parmesan muffins

The combination of butternut squash and Parmesan not only tastes delicious but also makes these easy muffins nutritious and satisfying. Eat within a day of baking.

MAKES 12

1 small butternut squash, about 400g (14oz),
  peeled, seeded and diced
1 red onion, peeled and finely chopped
1 tablespoon olive oil
75g (3oz) butter, melted
150g (5oz) Parmesan cheese, freshly grated, plus
  a little extra to sprinkle
225g (8oz) self-raising flour
4 eggs, beaten
3–4 tablespoons milk
sea salt and freshly ground black pepper

1 Preheat the oven to 200°C (fan oven 180°C), gas mark 6. Place the squash and onion on a baking sheet and drizzle over the olive oil. Season with salt and pepper and bake for 15 minutes until tender. Roughly mash on the baking sheet.

2 Lower the oven temperature to 180°C (fan oven 160°C), gas mark 4. Line a 12-hole muffin tin with squares of greaseproof paper (pushed in roughly) or with paper cases.

3 Spoon the pumpkin and onion mixture into a large bowl and stir in the melted butter, Parmesan, flour, eggs, milk and some salt and pepper to make a thick, lumpy batter. Divide the mixture among the cases and sprinkle over some extra Parmesan. Bake for 20–25 minutes until golden and just firm.

4 Transfer to a wire rack to cool. Serve warm or cool completely before packing into lunchboxes.

gorgeous cranberry cookies

These scrumptious biscuits really deserve their name – they're crunchy with a lovely buttery flavour and little nuggets of chewy dried cranberry. Store in an airtight container.

MAKES 24

175g (6oz) unsalted butter, at room temperature
150g (5oz) golden caster sugar
finely grated zest of 1 large orange
2 egg yolks
50g (2oz) ground almonds
50g (2oz) dried cranberries or cherries
225g (8oz) self-raising flour
2 tablespoons milk

1 Preheat the oven to 170°C (fan oven 150°C), gas mark 3. Using an electric mixer, beat together the butter and sugar until pale and creamy.

2 Stir in the orange zest, egg yolks, ground almonds, dried cranberries and flour. Mix well together, then roll into walnut-sized balls.

3 Place on a baking sheet, spaced well apart, and flatten each ball slightly with your hand. Brush with milk, then bake for 18–20 minutes until golden.

4 After removing from the oven, leave the cookies to firm up on the baking sheet for 5 minutes before transferring to a wire rack to cool.

caramel ripple brownies

These lovely rich, rippled brownies are fantastic served with coffee. As they are quite dense, cut them into small squares and wrap in foil for lunchboxes.

MAKES 16

100g (3¹/₂oz) luxury dark chocolate
100g (3¹/₂oz) unsalted butter
2 eggs, beaten
150g (5oz) light muscovado sugar
50g (2oz) plain flour

FOR THE CARAMEL RIPPLE:
200g (7oz) soft cheese
50g (2oz) dark muscovado sugar
few drops of vanilla extract
1 egg

1 Preheat the oven to 170°C (fan oven 150°C), gas mark 3. Line a 20cm (8 inch) square shallow cake tin with silicone paper or baking parchment.

2 Break up the chocolate into a heatproof bowl and add the butter. Set over a pan of gently simmering water and melt, stirring from time to time.

3 Meanwhile, prepare the caramel ripple mixture. Combine the soft cheese, muscovado sugar, vanilla extract and egg in a bowl and mix well until evenly blended. Set aside.

4 Stir the eggs and sugar into the chocolate mixture, then sift over the flour and gently fold in.

5 Spoon half of the chocolate mixture into the prepared tin, then alternately dollop teaspoonfuls of the caramel mixture and the remaining chocolate mixture on top. Using a chopstick or skewer, lightly ripple together to make a marbled top.

6 Bake for 25–30 minutes until just set. Leave to cool in the tin for 5–10 minutes before cutting into squares. Transfer to a wire rack to cool completely.

lemon custard tarts

Based on the fashionable and yummy Portuguese tarts, these tiny lemony mouthfuls, paired with a shot of hot black coffee, will really perk you up. Fortunately they are robust enough to tuck into school lunchboxes too.

MAKES 24
350g packet puff pastry, thawed if frozen
1 vanilla pod
300ml (½ pint) milk
1 egg

1 egg yolk
50g (2oz) caster sugar
25g (1oz) plain flour
grated zest and juice of ½ lemon
icing sugar, to dust (optional)

1 Preheat the oven to 200°C (fan oven 180°C), gas mark 6. Roll out the pastry as thinly as possible, then stamp out 24 x 7cm (2¾ inch) rounds. Use to line two 12-hole mini muffin tins.

2 Fill each pastry case with a dense ball of foil. Bake for 10–15 minutes until crisp and light golden, remove the foil and set aside. Lower the oven temperature to 170°C (fan oven 150°C), gas mark 3.

3 To make the filling, split the vanilla pod lengthways and place in a saucepan with the milk. Heat until almost boiling, then set aside for 10 minutes. Meanwhile, beat together the egg, egg yolk, sugar and flour in a bowl until smooth.

4 Remove the vanilla pod from the warm milk, then gradually pour on to the egg mixture. Return to a clean pan and stir over a medium heat until simmering. When the mixture begins to simmer, beat it quite vigorously to get rid of any lumps. Stir in the lemon zest and juice.

5 Divide the lemon filling among the pastry cases. Bake the tarts for 10–15 minutes until the custard filling has set. Leave in the tins for a few minutes, then carefully transfer to a wire rack to cool. Dust with icing sugar before serving if you like.

rough raspberry and almond slice

Here's a rustic – and pretty quick – version of a classic Bakewell tart. Having grown up in Derbyshire, I know the original (soggy) Bakewell pudding very well – I would rather tuck into one of these slices any day!

SERVES 8

500g (1lb 2oz) ready-made shortcrust pastry
50g (2oz) butter, at room temperature
50g (2oz) golden caster sugar
1 small egg
125g (4oz) ground almonds
few drops of vanilla extract
125g (4oz) raspberries
25g (1oz) flaked almonds
1 tablespoon icing sugar

1 Preheat the oven to 200°C (fan oven 180°C), gas mark 6. Roll out the pastry to a 30 x 20cm (12 x 8 inch) rectangle – don't worry if the edges aren't straight, as that's part of the charm. Transfer to a non-stick baking sheet and prick in several places. Bake for 5 minutes until set.

2 Meanwhile, using an electric mixer, beat the butter and caster sugar together until pale and fluffy. Stir in the egg, ground almonds and vanilla extract to make a stiff paste.

3 Spread the almond paste on top of the pastry, leaving a 1cm (½ inch) border clear on all sides. Gently press the raspberries into the paste. Scatter over the almonds and sift over the icing sugar. Bake for 20–25 minutes until puffed and golden.

4 Leave on the baking sheet for a few minutes, then carefully transfer to a wire rack to cool. Slice and serve warm, or at room temperature.

moist mango and maple cake

This classic teatime loaf cake is incredibly easy to make. It's reminiscent of a traditional carrot cake, so I've topped it with an old-fashioned cream cheese frosting. Wrap thick slices in greaseproof paper for picnics and lunchboxes.

SERVES 8

125g (4oz) butter
150g (5oz) light muscovado sugar
100g (3½oz) maple syrup
150g (5oz) plain flour
100g (3½oz) wholemeal flour
2 teaspoons baking powder
1 tablespoon ground cinnamon
2 ripe mangoes, peeled, stoned and
  finely chopped
100g (3½oz) pecan nuts, roughly chopped
FOR THE FROSTY TOPPING:
grated zest and juice of 1 small orange
200g (7oz) soft cheese
50g (2oz) icing sugar, sifted

1 Preheat the oven to 170°C (fan oven 150°C), gas mark 3. Gently melt the butter, sugar and maple syrup together in a small pan.

2 In a large bowl, mix together the flours, baking powder, cinnamon, mango and pecan pieces. Stir in the melted syrup mixture.

3 Spoon the mixture into a non-stick 500g (1lb) loaf tin that is about 16 x 10cm and 8cm deep (6½ x 4 inches and 3¼ inches deep). Bake for 1–1¼ hours until a skewer inserted into the centre of the cake comes out clean.

4 Leave the cake to cool in the tin for 5 minutes, then turn out on to a wire rack to cool completely.

5 For the topping, mix together the orange zest, soft cheese and icing sugar with enough of the orange juice to make a smooth, thick paste. Spread thickly over the top of the cooled cake. Cut into slices to serve.

5 just for two

tiger prawn tagliatelle

The perfect choice for a romantic supper for two, this is best made in the summer when tomatoes are at their tastiest. I've used fresh tagliatelle here, but you could always use dried pasta – add to a pan of boiling salted water at the beginning of step 1, and the sauce will be ready in the time it takes the pasta to cook.

SERVES 2

1 tablespoon olive oil
1 garlic clove, peeled and thinly sliced
3 ripe tomatoes, chopped
grated zest of 1 small lemon
squeeze of lemon juice
pinch of sugar
pinch of dried chilli flakes
200g (7oz) cooked, peeled tiger prawns
250g (9oz) fresh tagliatelle
2 tablespoons chopped flat leaf parsley
sea salt and freshly ground black pepper

1 Heat the olive oil in a small frying pan and cook the garlic for 1 minute until beginning to soften. Add the tomatoes and simmer gently for 5 minutes until they become pulpy.

2 Add the lemon zest and lemon juice, together with the sugar, chilli flakes and seasoning to taste. Stir to mix. Add the cooked prawns and cook gently for a couple of minutes until heated through.

3 Meanwhile, cook the pasta in a large pan of boiling salted water according to the packet instructions until *al dente* (tender, but firm to the bite).

4 Drain the pasta well and return to the pan. Add the prawn sauce and parsley, toss to mix, then divide between warm bowls and serve.

griddled tuna with fiery tomato salsa

Fresh tuna has a meaty texture and a mild flavour that's well matched with a wicked little salsa like this one. Serve with summer leaves or crusty bread.

SERVES 2

2 ripe tomatoes, roughly chopped
1 shallot, peeled and thinly sliced
1 small garlic clove, peeled and very thinly sliced
1 green chilli, finely chopped
pinch of dried chilli flakes
juice of 1 lime
2 tablespoons olive oil
2 fresh tuna steaks, each about 175g (6oz)
1 teaspoon cracked black peppercorns
2 tablespoons chopped mint or coriander
sea salt and freshly ground black pepper

1 Mix the tomatoes, shallot, garlic, fresh and dried chilli together in a bowl. Stir in the lime juice, 1 tablespoon olive oil and some salt and pepper. Set aside at room temperature for at least 5 minutes, or up to an hour.

2 Preheat a ridged griddle pan. Rub the rest of the olive oil over the tuna steaks. Sprinkle over the peppercorns and press them in lightly with your fingertips.

3 Cook the tuna for 2–3 minutes on each side until nicely browned but still slightly pink in the centre. Place on two warm plates. Stir the mint into the salsa, then spoon over and alongside the tuna.

potato stuffed poussins

I do like little poussins – especially for a smart supper for two. They don't have quite the flavour of a fully grown chicken, but take very well to some robust seasonings, such as lemon and rosemary, with a little chilli kick.

SERVES 2

1 large floury potato, such as Maris Piper or King
   Edward, about 225g (8oz), peeled and diced
1 tablespoon olive oil
3 rosemary sprigs
1 shallot, peeled and sliced
1 garlic clove, peeled and finely chopped
pinch of dried chilli flakes
1 lemon
2 poussins, each about 500g (1lb 2oz)
25g (1oz) butter, at room temperature
salt and freshly ground black pepper

1 Cook the potato in a pan of boiling salted water for 10–15 minutes until tender.

2 Preheat the oven to 200°C (fan oven 180°C), gas mark 6. Heat the oil in a small frying pan. Strip the leaves off one of the rosemary sprigs, roughly chop and add to the pan with the shallot and garlic. Cook for 5 minutes until softened, then remove from the heat and transfer to a shallow bowl.

3 Drain the potato, add to the bowl and crush roughly. Add the chilli flakes, then grate in about half the zest from the lemon. Add salt and pepper and leave to cool.

4 Meanwhile, cut four thin slices off the lemon. Loosen the skin on the breast of each poussin and slide a rosemary sprig and two lemon slices between the meat and the skin.

5 Spoon the mash into the poussin cavities, then rub the butter over the breasts. Season with salt and pepper and place side by side in a shallow roasting tin. Roast for 50 minutes to 1 hour until crisp, golden and cooked through. Serve whole, with simple vegetables.

hot lamb baguette with mint and lime

I love a hot sandwich and, although steak with fried onions and melting cheese is pretty hard to beat, this minty lamb version has an altogether fresher, more vibrant flavour. I spread the bread with redcurrant jelly because it cuts beautifully with the mint and lime, but creamed horseradish makes a surprisingly delicious alternative.

SERVES 2

4 thin boneless lamb leg steaks
1 teaspoon olive oil
2 x 20cm (8 inch) lengths of baguette
2 teaspoons redcurrant jelly
1 garlic clove, halved
20g (3/4oz) mint
1 lime, cut into wedges
sea salt and freshly ground black pepper

1 Preheat a ridged griddle pan. Brush the lamb with the olive oil and cook in the hot pan for about 2 minutes on each side.

2 Meanwhile, split the lengths of baguette and spread the redcurrant jelly on the bases.

3 Transfer the lamb steaks to a large plate and rub with the cut surface of the garlic. Season the lamb with salt and pepper to taste, then place two steaks inside each baguette. Roughly tear in the mint leaves, squeeze in a good measure of lime juice and serve warm.

Thai beef salad

This classic salad, which originated in north-east Thailand, is a standard in Thai restaurants but is very easy to make at home. The beef is only seared on the outside and should be served very rare, so don't be tempted to overcook it. Some steamed rice and an icy beer are all you need for a delicious and rather elegant supper.
Illustrated on previous page

SERVES 2
250g (9oz) beef fillet
1 teaspoon vegetable oil
juice of 1 lime
2 tablespoons Thai fish sauce
1 teaspoon caster sugar
1 shallot, peeled and very thinly sliced
1 garlic clove, peeled and finely chopped
2 tablespoons roughly chopped mint or coriander
1 Thai bird's eye chilli, thinly sliced
1 heart of romaine lettuce, roughly torn
large handful of bean sprouts

1 Heat a small non-stick frying pan. Rub the beef with the oil and place in the hot pan. Cook over a very high heat for 5 minutes, turning, until well browned all over. Transfer to a plate and leave to rest for 5 minutes.

2 For the dressing, mix the lime juice, fish sauce and caster sugar together in a bowl, then stir in the shallot, garlic, mint and chilli.

3 Pile the torn lettuce on to two serving plates, then scatter over the bean sprouts. Thinly slice the beef and arrange on top. Spoon over the dressing and serve.

stir-fried pork and ginger noodles

A zingy little stir-fry that's cooked and on the table in under 10 minutes. This is a standard of my friend and fellow food writer, Jenny White, who regularly knocks this up in our lunch break.

SERVES 2

1 tablespoon sunflower oil

200g (7oz) pork stir-fry strips

*4cm (1½ inch) piece of fresh root ginger, peeled
  and shredded*

4 spring onions, trimmed and shredded

1 red chilli, deseeded and thinly sliced

3 x 150g packets vacuum-packed udon noodles

2 tablespoons soy sauce

juice of 1 small orange

1 teaspoon oriental chilli oil

1 teaspoon wine vinegar

handful of basil leaves

1 Heat a wok, then add the oil. When hot, add the pork strips and stir-fry for 5 minutes. Add the ginger, spring onions, chilli and noodles and cook for a further 2 minutes.

2 Mix the soy sauce, orange juice, chilli oil and vinegar together in a bowl, then pour into the pan. Toss together well and cook for a further minute or so until piping hot.

3 Add the basil leaves, toss to mix, then divide the stir-fry between warm bowls and serve.

sausage and lentil casserole

I always keep a variety of dried lentils in stock as they're fantastic for stews and soups. The Puy lentil is considered more sophisticated than most. It does have a lovely texture and flavour, but if you're serving this dish for supper, you can use everyday brown or green lentils.

SERVES 2

1 teaspoon olive oil
6 pork sausages
1 small onion, peeled and roughly chopped
2 garlic cloves, peeled and roughly chopped
150g (5oz) Puy lentils
600ml (1 pint) hot chicken stock
1 large tomato, roughly chopped
1 teaspoon balsamic vinegar
3 tablespoons chopped flat leaf parsley
sea salt and freshly ground black pepper

1 Heat the olive oil in a sauté pan and cook the sausages, turning from time to time, for 5–8 minutes until golden on all sides. Add the onion and garlic and cook for 2–3 minutes until beginning to soften.

2 Add the lentils, stock and chopped tomato. Bring to the boil, then cover and simmer very gently for 40–45 minutes until the lentils are tender and most of the stock has been absorbed.

3 Stir in the balsamic vinegar and parsley and add salt and pepper to taste. Spoon into warm bowls and serve with crusty bread.

freezer dinners for two

Sometimes after a hectic day, you just don't have the time or energy to cook. But this doesn't mean you have to resort to ready meals or junk food. With a little forward planning, you can always have an appetising meal to hand in your freezer. Casseroles, stews, curries, soups and pasta sauces are perfect for making in larger quantities and freezing. All of the recipes featured here serve 4, so make one for dinner, eat two portions straightaway and freeze the rest to enjoy at a later date.

Allow the food to cool completely before transferring to a suitable freezer container, and make sure it has a well-fitting lid – food left open in the freezer will suffer from freezer burn and the texture and flavour will be ruined. Plastic food boxes, foil takeaway cartons and sealed freezer bags are all ideal for freezing food. Freeze for up to 2 months. Thaw overnight in the fridge and reheat thoroughly to serve.

▲ Greek-style baked lamb with potatoes

Heat 2 tbsp olive oil in a roasting tin and fry 1 large sliced onion and 4 chopped garlic cloves for 3–4 minutes; push to one side. Add 4 bone-in lamb leg or shoulder steaks and brown over a high heat for 2–3 minutes each side. Add 450g (1lb) peeled, diced potatoes and cook for 3 minutes. Add a 400g can cherry tomatoes, 300ml (½ pint) lamb stock, a bay leaf, 1 tsp dried oregano and 12 pitted black olives. Bake at 190°C, gas mark 5 for 30–40 minutes until the potatoes are tender.

Boston baked pork and beans

In a flameproof casserole, fry 700g (1½lb) diced belly pork in 1 tbsp oil for 5 minutes; remove. Fry 1 large diced onion and 2 chopped garlic cloves until tender. Stir in 600ml (1 pint) dry cider, 150ml (¼ pint) passata, 2 tbsp sun-dried tomato paste, 1 tbsp black treacle, 1 tbsp brown sugar, 1 tsp black mustard seeds, the pork, and a drained 400g can black-eyed beans. Season, cover and cook at 170°C, gas 3 for 1–1½ hours.

▲ courgette and mint soup

Heat 40g (1½oz) butter in a large saucepan and fry 1 finely chopped onion for 5 minutes until softened. Add 350g (12oz) sliced courgettes and cook for 2–3 minutes. Pour in 750ml (1¼ pints) vegetable stock and bring to a simmer. Season, cover and simmer for 10–15 minutes until the courgettes are tender. Stir in a good handful of chopped mint, cool slightly, then blend until smooth. Heat through gently to serve.

▲ quick coq au vin

Heat 2 tbsp oil in a large sauté pan. Fry 8 large chicken thighs for 4 minutes each side; remove. Add 4 chopped streaky bacon rashers, 8 peeled shallots and 225g (8oz) halved chestnut mushrooms; fry, stirring, for 5 minutes. Return the chicken, add 2 tbsp brandy and cook for 1 minute, then stir in 300ml (½ pint) red wine, 200ml (7fl oz) chicken stock, 2 tbsp tomato purée and a bay leaf. Season, cover and simmer gently for 15 minutes, then cook uncovered for 10 minutes.

ricotta and basil frittata

This frittata offers a delicious pairing of two key Italian ingredients – ricotta and basil. I've used the traditional southern Italian method of tearing some fresh white bread into the beaten eggs to give the frittata a firm, almost cake-like texture. Serve with a tomato and red onion salad, and good crusty bread.

SERVES 2

2 tablespoons olive oil
5 eggs
2 slices of white bread, crusts removed
1 garlic clove, peeled and crushed
20g (3/4oz) basil, finely chopped
150g (5oz) ricotta cheese
sea salt and freshly ground black pepper

1   Preheat the grill to high. Heat a splash of the olive oil in a 20cm (8 inch) frying pan. Beat the eggs in a large bowl, then tear in the white bread and season with salt and pepper. Pour into the pan and cook very gently for 5 minutes.

2   Meanwhile, in a pestle and mortar, pound together the garlic and basil to make a paste. Stir in the remaining olive oil and season with salt and pepper.

3   Drop spoonfuls of the ricotta on to the fritatta, then drizzle over the basil dressing. Cook for a further 2–3 minutes until the frittata is almost completely set, then finish cooking under the hot grill for 3–4 minutes until completely set and golden brown.

4   Slide the frittata out of the pan on to a board and cut into wedges to serve.

butter bean and mozzarella burgers

These juicy, succulent bean burgers have delicious pockets of molten mozzarella inside. Butter beans are the perfect beans for burgers as they have a lovely creamy texture and combine well with aromatics, such as spring onions and garlic.

SERVES 2

4 spring onions, trimmed and thickly sliced
1 garlic clove, peeled and thickly sliced
410g can butter beans, drained
100g (3¹/₂oz) fresh white breadcrumbs
150g (5oz) mozzarella cheese, drained and diced
1 egg yolk
pinch of cayenne pepper
2–3 tablespoons vegetable oil
sea salt and freshly ground black pepper

TO SERVE:
2 crusty rolls, split open
1 ripe tomato, sliced
mayonnaise

1 Put the spring onions and garlic into a food processor and whiz until finely chopped. Add the beans and whiz again to form a coarse purée. Add the breadcrumbs, mozzarella, egg yolk, cayenne and some salt and pepper. Pulse to form a stiff paste.

2 Shape the mixture into two even-sized burgers. Heat the oil in a heavy non-stick frying pan. Shallow-fry the burgers for 3–4 minutes on each side until golden – the cheese may ooze out and make the burgers stick a little, so make sure you use a good non-stick pan.

3 Drain the burgers on kitchen paper. Serve in the crusty rolls with a few slices of tomato and a good dollop of mayonnaise.

6 family feasts

roast salmon and goat's cheese salad

This is a smashing summery salad. With its mix of pinks and greens, it looks gorgeous when casually presented on a large platter. Prepare all the elements, such as the crostini and salmon, ahead of time and just assemble when ready to serve.

SERVES 12

1 baguette, cut into 1cm (1/2 inch) slices
3–4 tablespoons olive oil
6 pieces of salmon fillet, each about 250g (9oz)
2 romaine lettuces, sliced or torn into
  large pieces
1 large cucumber, peeled and thinly sliced
20g (3/4oz) mint, roughly torn
20g (3/4oz) chives, snipped
200g (7oz) cooked beetroot, thinly sliced
400g (14oz) medium soft goat's cheese

FOR THE DRESSING:
3 tablespoons olive oil
1 tablespoon red wine vinegar
pinch of caster sugar
sea salt and freshly ground black pepper

1 Preheat the oven to 220°C (fan oven 200°C), gas mark 7. Arrange the slices of bread on baking sheets and brush lightly with olive oil, then sprinkle with a little sea salt. Bake for 10–12 minutes until golden brown. Leave to cool on a wire rack, then pile these crostini on a serving board.

2 Arrange the salmon fillets on a baking sheet. Brush with a little olive oil and season with salt and pepper. Bake for 12–15 minutes until golden and just cooked. Leave to cool.

3 Scatter the lettuce on a large serving platter. Add the cucumber, mint, chives and beetroot. Crumble over the goat's cheese. Flake the salmon and scatter on top.

4 Mix together the dressing ingredients and drizzle over the salad. Serve fairly swiftly, with the crostini on the side.

smoked salmon tart

This is perfect for a family feast. Make two tarts the day before and keep in a cool, dry place – not the fridge or the pastry will go soggy. Serve with a simple salad for an elegant lunch.

SERVES 6

225g (8oz) plain flour
1/2 teaspoon salt
125g (41/2oz) chilled butter, diced
1 teaspoon dried chilli flakes
450ml (3/4 pint) double cream

2 large eggs
2 egg yolks
100g (31/2oz) Parmesan cheese, freshly grated
200g (7oz) smoked salmon, roughly torn
  into strips
sea salt and freshly ground black pepper

1 Preheat the oven to 200°C (fan oven 180°C), gas mark 6. Place the flour, salt, butter and chilli flakes in a food processor and whiz until the mixtures forms fine crumbs. Pour in 3 tablespoons very cold water and pulse again briefly, to form a firm dough.

2 Roll out the pastry on a floured surface and use to line a 22cm (81/2 inch) loose-bottomed flan tin. Use a rolling pin to lift the pastry into the tin. Press the pastry well into the sides, then trim away excess pastry overhanging the tin.

3 Prick the bottom of the pastry case with a fork, then fill with crumpled foil and bake for 10 minutes. Take the pastry case out of the oven and remove the foil. Lower the oven temperature to 180°C (fan oven 160°C), gas mark 4.

4 Beat together the cream, whole eggs and egg yolks until well blended. Stir in the Parmesan and smoked salmon and season with some salt and pepper. Pour into the pastry case. Bake for 25 minutes until the filling is just set.

5 Carefully remove the tart from the tin and cut into slices to serve while still warm.

quattro stagioni baking tray tart

Family occasions often involve catering for fussy eaters, so I've based this tart on the classic 'four seasons' pizza. With four different toppings, it looks pretty and should please everyone. Make two tarts for a larger gathering.
Illustrated on previous page

SERVES 4–6

500g packet puff pastry, thawed if frozen
2–3 tablespoons olive oil
8 tablespoons passata
large pinch of dried oregano
150g (5oz) mozzarella cheese, drained and diced
handful of basil leaves
sea salt and freshly ground black pepper

FOR TOPPING 1:
4 slices Parma ham, roughly torn
1 ripe fig, sliced

FOR TOPPING 2:
3–4 chestnut mushrooms, thinly sliced
1 garlic clove, peeled and thinly sliced

FOR TOPPING 3:
12 slices pepperoni
1 red chilli, thinly sliced

FOR TOPPING 4:
1 tablespoon black olives
6 anchovy fillets in oil, drained

1   Preheat the oven to 220°C (fan oven 200°C), gas mark 7. Roll out the pastry to a rectangle, about 40 x 25cm (16 x 10 inches) and place on a baking sheet. Using a small knife, score a 1cm (½ inch) border all around the edge, then prick the pastry within the border, using a fork.

2   Lightly brush the border with olive oil. Using the knife, score the rectangle into four even-sized quarters. Spoon the passata all over the pastry, staying with the border, then sprinkle with the oregano and some salt and pepper.

3   Arrange each topping on a quarter, then scatter over the mozzarella evenly, avoiding the olive and anchovy section. Drizzle with olive oil and season with salt and pepper. Bake for 20 minutes until puffed, crisp and golden.

4   Tear over the basil, then use a pizza wheel to slice off wedges. Serve with a simple salad.

prawn dupiaza with saffron rice

I have been told that dupiaza means 'double onions' and is simply a basic curry. I like to give mine a touch of sweetness with coconut, and sourness with fresh lemon. I think the simple saffron rice makes a lovely partner, but plain basmati will do just fine too.

SERVES 12

3 tablespoons sunflower oil

6 onions, peeled and thinly sliced

6 cardamom pods, cracked

1kg (2¼lb) tomatoes, roughly chopped

200g carton creamed coconut

600ml (1 pint) vegetable stock

6 tablespoons hot curry paste

1 tablespoon dark muscovado sugar

1.25kg (2¾lb) peeled raw tiger prawns,
   thawed if frozen

grated zest and juice of 1 lemon

sea salt and freshly ground black pepper

20g (¾oz) coriander, leaves only, to serve

FOR THE RICE:

pinch of saffron threads

25g (1oz) butter

1kg (2¼lb) basmati rice

1 teaspoon table salt

1 Preheat the oven to 180°C (fan oven 160°C), gas mark 4. Begin with the rice: stir the saffron into 2 litres (3½ pints) boiling water and set aside. Melt the butter in a large flameproof casserole, add the rice and stir to coat the grains in the butter. Cook for 1 minute, then pour in the saffron water and stir in the salt. Bring to the boil, then cover and transfer to the oven. Bake for 30 minutes until the rice is tender and the liquid has been absorbed.

2 Meanwhile, heat the oil in a roasting tin set on the hob and cook the onions for 15 minutes until softened and golden. Add the cardamom pods and tomatoes and cook gently for 10 minutes until the tomatoes are softened and pulpy.

3 Stir in the coconut, stock, curry paste, sugar and some salt and pepper. Bring to a gentle simmer and cook for 25 minutes, adding a little water if the sauce seems too thick.

4 Stir in the prawns with the lemon zest and juice, and cook for a further 2–3 minutes until the prawns are just cooked.

5 Divide the rice among warm plates, spoon the curry on top (there should be plenty of sauce), and scatter over the coriander leaves to serve.

oriental roast chicken

This simple but flavoursome and aromatic dish looks stunning when brought to the table on a platter. You can use one very large roasting tin or two smaller ones. I like to buy whole chickens and cut them into quarters so I get a mixture of breasts and legs, plus some wings and bones to make chicken stock later. Of course, you can buy the pieces already prepared if you prefer.

SERVES 12

3 large chickens, each about 2kg (4½lb),
   quartered
4 garlic cloves, peeled and roughly chopped
4 shallots, peeled and roughly chopped
4cm (1½ inch) piece of fresh root ginger,
   peeled and roughly chopped
4 lemon grass stalks, roughly chopped

3 tablespoons light muscovado sugar
2 tablespoons Thai fish sauce
300ml (½ pint) chicken stock
juice of 1 lime
sea salt and freshly ground black pepper
6 spring onions, trimmed and thinly sliced,
   to serve

1 Deeply slash each chicken quarter 2 or 3 times and nestle them into a large roasting tin.

2 Pound the garlic, shallots, ginger, lemon grass and 2 tablespoons of the sugar together, using a pestle and mortar to make a coarse paste. Stir in the fish sauce. Rub the mixture over the chicken pieces, making sure it goes into the slashes. Leave in a cool place for at least 2 hours (ideally overnight in the fridge), turning from time to time.

3 Preheat the oven to 200°C (fan oven 180°C), gas mark 6. Sprinkle the chicken quarters with some coarse sea salt and roast for 45–50 minutes until beautifully crisp and brown, and cooked through. To check, insert a skewer into the thickest part of the thigh; the juices should run clear and not at all pink. When the chicken is cooked, transfer to a warmed large serving platter and set aside in a warm spot to rest for 5 minutes.

4 Pour away any fat from the roasting tin, then place the tin on the hob and pour in the stock. Bring to the boil, stirring to loosen any residue from the bottom of the tin. Simmer for a couple of minutes, then add the lime juice and the remaining sugar, to taste.

5 Pour the sauce over the chicken, scatter with spring onions and serve with rice and steamed Chinese greens.

Moroccan chicken and pastina bake

Small pasta shapes are very popular in North Africa and the addition of cinnamon, cumin and orange gives this dish a typical Middle Eastern flavour. It's a big, hearty family bake, and as it cooks the top of the pasta becomes golden and a little crunchy. The recipe uses a very large roasting tin, but if you haven't got one, simply use two regular tins.
Illustrated on previous page

SERVES 10

500g (1lb 2oz) cherry tomatoes
10 chicken thighs
1 garlic bulb, broken into cloves
1 tablespoon olive oil
1 large red onion, peeled and thinly sliced
700g (1 1/2lb) conchigliette, or other tiny
  dried pasta shapes
2 cinnamon sticks, broken in half
1 teaspoon cumin seeds
2 litres (3 1/2 pints) hot chicken stock
grated zest and juice of 1 large orange
20g (3/4oz) flat leaf parsley, roughly chopped
sea salt and freshly ground black pepper

1 Preheat the oven to 200°C (fan oven 180°C), gas mark 6. Put the cherry tomatoes into a large roasting tin and nestle the chicken thighs and garlic cloves among them. Drizzle over the olive oil and season with salt and pepper. Bake for 15 minutes.

2 Scatter the red onion slices over the chicken and bake for a further 5 minutes.

3 Now stir in the pasta, cinnamon, cumin, stock, orange zest and juice, and a little more seasoning. Return to the oven and bake for a further 15–20 minutes or until the pasta is cooked and the liquid has been absorbed. Stir through the chopped parsley and serve straight from the tin.

minted chicken and new potato salad

This is ideal for outdoor eating – chicken, new potatoes and green beans are tossed in a minty yogurt dressing for the perfect summer salad. Most supermarkets sell whole roasted chickens. For this recipe, I recommend you buy a plain one (rather than a flavoured chicken), or better still, roast your own side by side in a large roasting tin. A 1.5kg (3¼lb) chicken will take about 1 hour, 25 minutes at 200°C (fan oven 180°C), gas mark 6.

SERVES 12

2 roast chickens, each about 1.5kg (3¼lb)

1.5kg (3¼lb) baby new potatoes, halved if large

250g (9oz) fine green beans, trimmed

4 tablespoons pine nuts, toasted

1 bunch of spring onions, trimmed and sliced

FOR THE MINTY DRESSING:
3 tablespoons Greek yogurt

3 tablespoons olive oil

pinch of sugar

20g (¾oz) mint

sea salt and freshly ground black pepper

1   Remove the legs and breasts from the roast chickens. Tear the breast meat into bite-sized pieces and place in a large wide serving bowl. Remove the leg meat from the bones and tear it into similar pieces; add to the bowl. Strip any meat from the chicken carcasses and add this too. Set aside.

2   Cook the potatoes in boiling salted water for 10–12 minutes until tender. Add the beans for the last 2–3 minutes of cooking. Drain well and cool under cold running water. Drain and pat dry on kitchen paper. Add to the chicken together with the pine nuts and spring onions and mix well.

3   To make the dressing, whisk together the yogurt, olive oil, 3 tablespoons water, sugar and some salt and pepper. Set aside a few mint leaves to garnish; finely chop the rest and stir into the dressing.

4   Pour the dressing over the salad, tossing to make sure everything is coated. Scatter with the reserved mint leaves and serve.

vegetable accompaniments

A vegetable accompaniment should be as flavourful and interesting as the main course. Even something like a humble jacket potato can be turned into a delicious side dish – try baking whole sweet potatoes in their skins and serving with a garlic and chilli butter.

We have an enormous array of vegetables available to us in this country, and it's best to try to use those in season. Asparagus is available all year round now, but it's flavour in November will never match that of English asparagus, which is found only during May and June. In the winter months, when seasonal vegetables seem limited and boring, there are many ways to pep them up, such as stir-frying shredded cabbage with cumin seeds and toasted sesame oil, or roasting carrots with garlic. Broccoli is always popular and it's easy to liven up with a few flavourings. Each of the following accompaniments serves 4–6, but you can easily double or triple up the quantities.

▲ **roasted carrots with garlic**
Scrub 500g (1lb 2oz) carrots, then cut into 1 cm (½ inch) thick slices. Place in a roasting tin with a splash of olive oil and a little salt and caster sugar. Toss to mix and roast in the oven at 190°C, gas 5 for 15 minutes. Scatter over a handful of whole, unpeeled garlic cloves and roast for a further 30 minutes until tender and golden brown. Add a splash of balsamic vinegar and some chopped parsley to serve.

clapshot (tatties and neeps)

Peel 500g (1lb 2oz) each of swede and floury potatoes, cut into chunks and boil until tender. Meanwhile, cook 2 snipped streaky bacon rashers in a dry frying pan until crisp and golden, then add 4 thinly sliced spring onions and cook for 1 minute. Drain the swede and potatoes and mash well. Beat in the bacon and spring onions, together with a splash of warm milk. Season with salt and pepper to taste and serve.

sesame, green bean and radish salad

Blanch 450g (1lb) fine green beans in boiling salted water for 2–3 minutes, then drain and refresh under cold running water. Sauté a thinly sliced garlic clove in 3 tbsp sunflower oil until just turning golden, then transfer to a bowl and whisk with 2 tsp toasted sesame oil and 1 tbsp light soy sauce. Combine the beans and 5 thinly sliced radishes in a serving dish and pour over the dressing. Scatter with some toasted sesame seeds and serve.

▲ long stem broccoli with chilli and lemon

Trim the base of the stalk from a head of broccoli, then cut into long florets, leaving a good length of stalk on each. Cook the broccoli in a pan of boiling salted water for 2 minutes, then drain. Heat a splash of sunflower oil in a non-stick frying pan and cook 1 or 2 thinly sliced garlic cloves for a few seconds. Add the broccoli and 1 or 2 sliced red chillies, and stir-fry for 2–3 minutes until tender but still firm. Squeeze in the juice of ½ lemon and add some salt and pepper.

succulent pork roast

This is based on a classic Italian dish known as *porchetta*. I find that shoulder of pork is the best cut to use as it has exactly the right balance of meat and fat. The pork is best served warm, but not straight from the oven.

SERVES 10–12

20g (¾oz) rosemary sprigs
1 boneless shoulder of pork, about 4kg (9lb)
50g (2oz) Parmesan cheese, freshly grated
4 garlic cloves, peeled and finely chopped
40g (1½oz) flat leaf parsley, chopped
sea salt and freshly ground black pepper

1 If you want the pork to have a soft, chewy skin, which is traditional for this dish, then preheat the oven now to 190°C (fan oven 170°C), gas mark 5.

2 Remove the leaves from 2 sprigs of rosemary and roughly chop. Cut the strings on the pork and open it out on a flat surface. Season generously with salt and pepper, then evenly sprinkle over the Parmesan, garlic and chopped rosemary and parsley.

3 Roll up the pork again to enclose the filling. Tie with string at 2cm (¾ inch) intervals to keep the meat in shape. If the skin is not already scored, use a small very sharp knife to score it between the strings. Sprinkle with salt, then slip the remaining rosemary sprigs under the strings.

4 For a soft, chewy skin, roast the pork straight away, allowing 20 minutes per 500g (1lb 2oz) plus 20 minutes – if your joint weighs 4kg (9lb), it will take 3 hours. If you want the pork to have a crunchy crackling (which will make it harder to carve), leave it for at least 2 hours before cooking. Then, before putting it in to roast, pat with kitchen paper to dry off the excess water. Roast at the same temperature, turning up the oven to 220°C (fan oven 200°C), gas mark 7 for the last 20 minutes of the cooking time.

5 Leave the pork to rest for a good 30 minutes before carving. If you've got an electric carving knife at the back of a cupboard somewhere, then this is the perfect time to get it out.

crusty-topped shepherds pie

An absolute winner on any family table. This version has a little extra zing from the caraway seeds and it's all topped off with a delicious Cheddar mash.

SERVES 12

3 tablespoons olive oil
3 onions, peeled and chopped
4 garlic cloves, peeled and chopped
4 carrots, peeled and diced
2 teaspoons caraway seeds
1.5kg (3¼lb) lean lamb mince
1 small Savoy cabbage, sliced
1.5 litres (2½ pints) chicken stock
6 tablespoons brown sauce
300g (11oz) frozen peas
20g (¾oz) flat leaf parsley, roughly chopped

FOR THE CHEDDAR MASH:

2kg (4½lb) floury potatoes such as Maris Piper
    or King Edward, peeled and cubed
150ml (¼ pint) milk
50g (2oz) butter
250g (9oz) mature Cheddar cheese, grated
sea salt and freshly ground black pepper

1 Heat the olive oil in a large roasting tin set on the hob. Add the onions, garlic, carrots and caraway seeds and cook for 3–4 minutes. Add the mince and cook for a further 5–10 minutes, stirring now and again, until browned.

2 Drain off any excess fat, then stir in the cabbage and cook for another couple of minutes. Add the stock and brown sauce. Bring to the boil, then simmer very gently for 30 minutes.

3 Meanwhile, make the mash. Cook the potatoes in boiling salted water for 15–20 minutes until tender. Drain well, then mash and stir in the milk, butter, cheese and seasoning.

4 Preheat the oven to 180°C (fan oven 160°C), gas mark 4. Stir the peas and parsley into the mince and season with salt and pepper. Spread out smoothly, then spoon over the mash and rough up the surface with the back of a spoon. Bake for 45 minutes until bubbling and golden.

roast shoulder of lamb with sticky pancetta potatoes

When it comes to roasting meat it's always best to have it at room temperature. So a couple of hours before roasting, take the lamb out of the fridge and dress with the marinade. You will need to ask the butcher to leave the shoulder whole for this dish. For large feasts, quantities can easily be doubled.

SERVES 6–8

1 whole shoulder of lamb, about 2.5kg (5½lb)
2 garlic cloves, peeled and finely chopped
20g (¾oz) mint, finely chopped
1 teaspoon dried oregano
3 tablespoons olive oil
1.5–2kg (3¼–4½lb) red skinned potatoes,
  such as Desirée, scrubbed
125g (4oz) cubed pancetta
2 red onions, thinly sliced
100ml (3½fl oz) dry cider
sea salt and freshly ground black pepper

1 First weigh the lamb to estimate the cooking time – it needs 30 minutes per kilo (2¼ lb) plus 20 minutes, so for a 2.5kg (5½lb) joint, you will need to cook it for 1 hour and 35 minutes.

2 Place the lamb on a rack set over a roasting tin. Using a skewer, deeply pierce the meat in several places. Stir together the garlic, mint, oregano, olive oil and some salt and pepper. Brush all over the lamb, then set aside for at least an hour.

3 Preheat the oven to 200°C (fan oven 180°C), gas mark 6. Cook the whole potatoes in a pan of boiling salted water for 15 minutes. Drain, then cut into 2cm (¾ inch) thick slices.

4 Lift the lamb on its rack off the roasting tin and scatter the sliced potatoes, pancetta and red onion into the tin. Season with salt and pepper and pour over the cider. Replace the rack and roast the lamb according to your calculations.

5 Transfer the lamb to a warm platter and leave to rest in a warm spot for 15 minutes before carving. Turn the oven off and put the tin of potatoes back in to keep warm while the meat is resting. Serve the lamb with the sticky pancetta potatoes.

boiled beef and carrots with herb dumplings

This is a proper old-fashioned, warming stew and so I've chosen to use lard as the cooking fat. If you prefer you can substitute a couple of tablespoons of vegetable oil. I don't have a casserole dish big enough so I use a sturdy, deep roasting tin, but if you happen to have a very large casserole, do use it.

SERVES 10

40g (1½oz) lard

2kg (4½lb) chuck steak, cut into large cubes

4 tablespoons plain flour

4 onions, peeled and sliced

1.5kg (3¼lb) carrots, peeled and thickly sliced

2 bay leaves

3 rosemary sprigs

500ml (16fl oz) red wine

1.5 litres (2½ pints) hot beef stock

sea salt and freshly ground black pepper

FOR THE DUMPLINGS:

250g (9oz) self-raising flour

1 teaspoon baking powder

½ teaspoon table salt

125g (4½oz) suet

20g (¾oz) flat leaf parsley or chives, finely chopped

1 Preheat the oven to 170°C (fan oven 150°C), gas mark 3. Set the roasting tin on the hob and add the lard to melt.

2 Meanwhile, toss the meat in the flour to coat lightly. Add to the tin and cook for 10 minutes, stirring fairly frequently, until nicely browned. Remove and set aside.

3 Add the onions to the roasting tin and brown them, then add the carrots, bay leaves, rosemary, wine and stock. Return the browned beef and add some seasoning. Bring to the boil. Cover with foil and transfer to the oven to cook for 2 hours until the meat is tender.

4 To make the dumplings, place the flour in a large bowl and stir in the baking powder, salt, suet and herbs. Stir in enough water – about 150ml (¼ pint) – to make a soft dough. Don't worry if it's a little sticky. Roll into 20 balls, each about the size of a cherry.

5 Drop the dumplings into the stew and continue cooking, still covered for 30–35 minutes until the dumplings are puffed and cooked through.

7 puddings

lemonade granita

This is the perfect do-ahead dessert. The balance of sugar, acidic lemon and water means that it freezes into a beautifully textured granita. It will keep in the freezer for weeks, but may then need a firm hand to break up the crystals.
Illustrated left

SERVES 6
175g (6oz) caster sugar
grated zest and juice of 6 lemons
1 lemon grass stalk, roughly flattened with a
   rolling pin
450ml (3/4 pint) soda water

1   Put the sugar, lemon zest and juice, and lemon grass stalk into a saucepan with 150ml (1/4 pint) water. Heat gently, stirring, until the sugar dissolves, then simmer gently for 5 minutes. Leave to cool.

2   Strain the liquid into a rigid container and stir in the soda water. Freeze for 2 hours until almost firm, then use a fork to break the mixture into large flaky crystals. Freeze for a further 2 hours, then break up again. Spoon into small tumblers for serving.

frozen berry yogurt and meringue pots

A simple fruit ice with nuggets of melt-in-the-mouth meringue, this is incredibly easy to prepare.
Illustrated on page 95

MAKES 6
75g (3oz) icing sugar
250g (9oz) frozen summer berries
4 tablespoons blackcurrant cordial
500g (1lb 2oz) Greek yogurt
2 meringue nests, crumbled

1   Sift the icing sugar over the frozen fruit, then drizzle over the blackcurrant cordial. Roughly break up the fruit with a fork.

2   Tip the yogurt into a bowl and beat with a wooden spoon to soften. Ripple through the fruit mixture with the crumbled meringues.

3   Spoon into six small freezerproof glasses and freeze for 2–3 hours until firm. If you freeze for longer than this, take the pots out of the freezer 10–20 minutes before serving, to soften up.

Bellini jellies

Here the classic Venetian cocktail is made into a gently wobbling dessert. Make ahead and serve as the ultimate dinner party finale, or between courses as a palate cleanser.

SERVES 6
600ml (1 pint) dry white wine
175g (6oz) caster sugar
5 sheets of leaf gelatine

1 large peach
4 tablespoons peach schnapps
1 pink rose

1 Place the wine and sugar in a small pan and simmer gently, stirring, until the sugar dissolves.

2 Meanwhile, soak the gelatine leaves in a shallow dish of cold water until softened, then drain and squeeze out the excess water. Remove the wine from the heat, add the gelatine leaves and stir until melted. Set aside to cool.

3 Cut a cross in the skin at the base of the peach, then plunge into boiling water. Leave for 1 minute, then remove. Using a small knife, peel off all the skin. Halve, remove the stone and roughly chop the flesh. Purée in a mini chopper until smooth, then pass through a sieve.

4 Once the wine is at room temperature, stir in the peach purée and schnapps, then pour into six moulds or ramekins. Carefully pull some of the petals from the rose and float a couple of rose petals on each jelly. Chill for at least 3 hours until set.

5 To serve, dip the moulds briefly into hot water, then turn out the jellies on to small plates. Decorate with more rose petals (and the rosebud if you like).

little apricot and lavender mousses

Make these light-as-air fruit mousses in early summer when fragrant fresh apricots are in season.

SERVES 6

1kg (2¼lb) apricots, stoned and roughly
   chopped
125g (4oz) caster sugar

½ teaspoon lavender flowers or 2 rosemary sprigs
1 sheet of leaf gelatine
1 egg white
150ml (¼ pint) double cream

1   Combine the apricots, caster sugar, lavender and 5 tablespoons water in a saucepan. Cook gently for 15–20 minutes, stirring from time to time, until the fruit is pulpy and almost smooth.

2   Soak the leaf gelatine in a shallow dish of cold water until softened, then drain and squeeze out the excess water. Remove the apricot mixture from the heat and stir in the leaf gelatine, until melted. Leave to cool. (If you used rosemary in place of the lavender, remove the sprig at this stage.)

3   Whisk the egg white until it forms firm peaks. Whip the cream in another bowl until thick. Fold the egg white and cream into the cooled apricot mixture. Spoon into individual pots or glasses and chill for at least 2 hours until nicely set.

coffee cream trifle

This simple trifle needs a night in the fridge so it's perfect as a make-ahead dinner party dessert. Overnight the sugar melts into the cream, leaving a scrumptious syrupy layer on the surface.

SERVES 8

150g (5oz) cantuccini biscuits
100ml (3½fl oz) strong black coffee
4 tablespoons Marsala or dessert wine
300ml (½ pint) double cream
500g (1lb 2oz) Greek yogurt
6 tablespoons demerara sugar

1   Break the biscuits roughly into a glass serving bowl and pour over the coffee and Marsala. Leave to soak for 10 minutes or so.

2   Meanwhile, whip the cream until it forms soft peaks, then stir in the yogurt. Spoon over the biscuits and sprinkle the sugar on top. Cover and chill overnight.

panettone bruschetta with summer fruit compote

This most spectacular summer dessert of sugar-toasted slices of panettone topped with juicy soft fruits can double as a brilliant breakfast.

SERVES 4

150ml (¼ pint) freshly squeezed orange juice
1 vanilla pod, halved lengthways
1 star anise
50g (2 oz) caster sugar
300g (11 oz) mixed summer fruits, such as
   raspberries, strawberries and blueberries
4 large slices of panettone
50g (2 oz) butter, melted
2 tablespoons icing sugar
4 tablespoons Greek yogurt or extra thick cream

1 Heat the orange juice in a small pan with the split vanilla pod, star anise and caster sugar. Bring to a gentle boil, then remove from the heat. Stir in the fruit and leave to cool completely, then chill until ready to serve.

2 Preheat a griddle pan. Brush the panettone with the melted butter, then dust with icing sugar. Toast on the griddle pan for 1–2 minutes on each side until crisp and golden brown.

3 Divide the griddled panettone among four plates and spoon over the fruit compote, discarding the vanilla pod and star anise. Top each portion with a spoonful of yogurt and serve.

effortless puddings

Most of us like a little something sweet at the end of a meal, but without a lot of fuss. When a piece of fruit just isn't enough, or when you've planned a busy dinner party and want to save time on the pudding, make good use of simple ingredients and quality convenience foods. With these you can turn out an impressive and satisfying dessert in a matter of minutes.

Stir together creamy ingredients such as mascarpone or softly whipped cream with strawberries mashed with icing sugar to make a speedy fruit fool. This needs only a shortbread biscuit alongside.

Many fruits, including rhubarb, plums and peaches, can be baked to good effect: dot with a little butter and add a sprinkling of sugar and spice, then bake until tender (up to 30 minutes depending on the fruit you choose). Serve with a scoop of vanilla ice cream or a dollop of crème fraîche. Or try one of the following speedy ideas.

▲ **raspberry slush**

To serve 4, put 250g (9oz) frozen raspberries into a food processor with 4 tbsp lime cordial and 200–250ml (7–9fl oz) lemonade. Whiz to form a coarse slush. Pour into glasses and serve immediately.

stir-fried toffee pineapple

To serve 3–4, drain a 432g can pineapple chunks and pat dry on kitchen paper. Heat a large knob of butter in a frying pan and add the pineapple, 2 tbsp light soft brown sugar and 2 tbsp desiccated coconut. Cook over a high heat for 4–5 minutes until golden brown. Serve straightaway, with scoops of vanilla ice cream.

chocolate banana cups

To serve 6, melt 200g (7oz) luxury dark chocolate in the microwave or in a bowl set over a pan of simmering water. Pour a 500g carton fresh custard into a large bowl and, using an electric mixer, gradually whisk in the chocolate until smooth and well blended. Stir in 2 chopped bananas (or a bag of Maltesers if you prefer), then pour into six cups or glasses. If you have time, place in the fridge to chill and set.

▲ blueberry pancakes

To serve 4, whisk together 2 eggs and 5 tbsp milk. Combine 150g (5oz) plain flour, 2 tbsp caster sugar and a pinch of salt in a large bowl. Make a well in the centre, pour in the egg mixture and beat with a whisk until smooth. Stir in 125g (4oz) blueberries. Heat just a tiny splash of sunflower oil in a non-stick pan. Add spoonfuls of the mixture and cook for 1–2 minutes on each side until puffed and golden. Stack and serve drizzled with maple syrup and/or single cream.

strawberry clafoutis

Although this is an incredibly simple dessert, it looks very stylish, which makes it perfect for entertaining. The idea came from my friend, chef Paul Merret, who makes this with juicy fresh peach cubes. I love to eat warm clafoutis topped with a scoop of melting ice cream.
Illustrated on previous page

SERVES 4
4 eggs
150g (5oz) caster sugar
150ml (¼ pint) double cream
1 tablespoon plain flour
1 tablespoon ground almonds
grated zest of 1 lime
225g (8oz) strawberries, halved if large

1 Preheat the oven to 190°C (fan oven 170°C), gas mark 5. Using an electric mixer, beat the eggs with the sugar until really thick and voluminous.

2 Lightly whip the cream until it forms soft peaks. Fold the cream into the egg mixture together with the flour, ground almonds and lime zest.

3 Divide the strawberries among four heatproof bowls or individual gratin dishes. Spoon over the batter and bake for 12 minutes until golden. Serve warm topped with a scoop of vanilla ice cream.

melting chocolate risotto

What could be better than rice pudding? Chocolate rice pudding! This one's an absolute stunner.

SERVES 6
750ml (1¼ pints) milk
50g (2oz) light muscovado sugar
50g (2oz) butter
½ teaspoon ground cinnamon
125g (4oz) risotto rice, such as Carnaroli
  or Arborio
100g (3½oz) luxury dark chocolate,
  roughly chopped

1   Put the milk and muscovado sugar into a pan and heat gently until the sugar dissolves.

2   Melt the butter in a large non-stick pan and stir in the cinnamon and rice. Cook for 1 minute, then add half of the hot sugared milk. Cook for 10 minutes, stirring from time to time. Pour in the remaining hot milk and stir and cook for a further 8–10 minutes until the rice is tender and the milk has been absorbed.

3   Scatter over the chocolate and stir to ripple through roughly. Spoon into bowls and serve warm. Alternatively, spoon into glasses and chill before serving.

soggy belly chocolate fudge cake

Here is a scrummy cross between a classic chocolate cake and a fudgy-centred brownie. It is best eaten on the day it's made, while still warm, which shouldn't be too much trouble. Serve with pouring cream or vanilla ice cream.

SERVES 8
200g (7oz) luxury dark chocolate
140g (4½oz) butter
3 tablespoons Irish cream liqueur or whiskey
5 eggs, separated

200g (7oz) vanilla caster sugar or regular
  caster sugar
100g (3½oz) plain flour
1 teaspoon baking powder

1   Preheat the oven to 180°C (fan oven 160°C), gas mark 4. Line a 23cm (9 inch) springform cake tin with silicone paper or baking parchment.

2   Put the chocolate, butter and liqueur into a large heatproof bowl set over a pan of gently simmering water and heat until melted. Remove from the heat and allow to cool for a couple of minutes. Stir until smooth.

3   Meanwhile, whisk the egg whites in a clean bowl until they form soft peaks. Gradually whisk in the sugar, a tablespoonful at a time.

4   Stir the eggs yolks into the chocolate mixture, then fold in the whisked egg white mixture. Sift over the flour and baking powder, and gently fold in using a large metal spoon.

5   Pour the mixture into the prepared tin and bake for 30–40 minutes until just set. Leave to cool in the tin for at least 20 minutes, then gently lift out of the tin and cut into wedges to serve.

best ever vanilla cheesecake

Most cheesecakes are good but, with its fantastic texture and light lemon and vanilla flavour, this one is unbeatable. Keep it in the fridge and cut slices off it all week.

SERVES 10
200g (7oz) gingernut biscuits
50g (2oz) butter, melted
1 vanilla pod
3 x 250g tubs mascarpone cheese
125g (4oz) caster sugar
2 tablespoons cornflour
3 eggs
grated zest of 1 lemon

1   Preheat the oven to 180°C (fan oven 160°C), gas mark 4. Put the biscuits into a strong polythene bag and crush with a rolling pin. Tip into a large bowl. Stir in the melted butter until evenly mixed.

2   Turn the crumb mixture into a 23cm (9 inch) non-stick springform cake tin, pressing the crumbs down firmly with the back of a spoon. Place in the fridge to chill for 5–10 minutes.

3   Using a small knife, slit open the vanilla pod and scrape the seeds into a large bowl. Add the mascarpone, sugar, cornflour, eggs and lemon zest, and beat with an electric mixer until smooth.

4   Pour the mixture into the cake tin and place on a baking sheet. Bake for 45 minutes or until golden – the filling will still be a little wobbly at this stage. Turn off the oven, open the door and leave the cheesecake inside until completely cool – the filling will set as it cools. Cut into wedges to serve.

snowy saffron peaches

Roasting really brings out the natural sweetness of ripe peaches. The snowy saffron meringues finish them off with a stylish flourish. Serve with vanilla ice cream.

SERVES 6

50g (2oz) butter

6 large, ripe peaches, halved

1 tablespoon roughly chopped pistachio nuts

65g (2½oz) caster sugar

small pinch of saffron threads

1 egg white

1 Preheat the oven to 200°C (fan oven 180°C), gas mark 6. Melt the butter in a small roasting tin in the oven, then put in the peach halves in one layer. Scatter in the nuts. Roast for 25 minutes, turning from time to time, until the peaches are tender and golden.

2 Meanwhile, whiz the caster sugar with the saffron in a mini chopper or blender until well blended. Whisk the egg white in a clean bowl to stiff peaks, then gradually whisk in the saffron sugar to make a firm, glossy meringue.

3 Turn the peach halves hollow side up. Spoon a peak of meringue on top of each one. Return to the oven to bake for 5 minutes until lightly tinged with brown. Serve hot, with the pan juices drizzled round.

treacle tart

Could there possibly be a better accompaniment to a cup of afternoon tea than this? The sweetness of the syrup and the zesty bite of lemon never fail to please.

SERVES 10

225g (8oz) plain flour
150g (5oz) cold butter, diced
1 egg yolk
1 teaspoon golden caster sugar

FOR THE FILLING:
800g (1¾lb) golden syrup
125g (4oz) fresh white breadcrumbs
finely grated zest of 2 lemons
50g (2oz) porridge oats
2 eggs, beaten

1   Preheat the oven to 180°C (fan oven 160°C), gas mark 4. Put the flour and butter into a food processor and pulse until the mixture forms fine crumbs. Add the egg yolk, sugar and 2 tablespoons cold water and pulse again briefly until the mixture comes together into a dough.

2   Roll out the dough on a lightly floured surface and use to line a fluted, deep, loose-bottomed 24cm (9½ inch) flan tin. Prick the bottom and chill for 30 minutes.

3   To make the filling, warm the golden syrup in a pan until runny but not too hot. Remove from the heat and stir in the breadcrumbs, lemon zest, oats and beaten eggs.

4   Pour the filling into the pastry case. Bake for 30–40 minutes until the filling is golden and just set; don't worry if it is still a little soft. Leave to cool in the tin for a few minutes, then carefully lift out. Cut into slices to serve.

old-fashioned coconut and jam tart

A wonderful moist tart, this has a classic 'teatime'-style layer of red jam between the pastry and coconut filling. It beats any shop bought version hands down.

SERVES 8

375g (13oz) ready-made sweet shortcrust pastry
3 eggs
125g (4oz) golden caster sugar
200ml carton coconut cream
75g (3oz) desiccated coconut
75g (3oz) plain flour
4 tablespoons seedless raspberry jam

1   Preheat the oven to 200°C (fan oven 180°C), gas mark 6. Roll out the pastry on a lightly floured surface and use to line a fluted, deep, loose-bottomed 24cm (9½ inch) flan tin. If you have time, rest in the fridge for 30 minutes. Prick the pastry lightly with a fork, fill with crumpled foil and bake for 15 minutes until set.

2   Using an electric mixer, beat the eggs and sugar together until thick and voluminous. Gently stir in the coconut cream, desiccated coconut and flour.

3   Reduce the oven temperature to 180°C (fan oven 160°C), gas mark 4. Lift the foil out of the pastry case, then spread the jam over the bottom. Pour in the coconut mixture.

4   Bake for 30–40 minutes until the filling is set and golden. Leave to cool in the tin for a few minutes, then carefully lift out, slice and serve.

oaty ginger pear crumble

Crumble is one of the easiest and most comforting puds ever made. The stem ginger in this filling gives every mouthful a little zing.

SERVES 8

8 dessert pears, such as Rocha
50g (2oz) butter
50g (2oz) light muscovado sugar
4 pieces of stem ginger in syrup, drained
  and finely chopped
juice of 1 lemon
FOR THE CRUMBLE TOPPING:
150g (5oz) cold butter, diced
300g (11oz) plain flour
100g (3¹/₂oz) rolled oats
175g (6oz) light muscovado sugar

1 Preheat the oven to 180°C (fan oven 160°C), gas mark 4. Peel, quarter and core the pears, then cut into chunks. Put the butter into a pan with the pears, sugar, ginger and lemon juice and cook gently for 10 minutes.

2 Meanwhile, make the crumble topping. Rub the butter into the flour until there are no large pieces left. Stir in the oats and sugar.

3 Spoon the fruit mixture into a large ovenproof dish and scatter over the crumble mixture. Bake for 40–45 minutes until nicely browned. Serve with hot custard.

index

a

almonds: rough raspberry and almond slice, 122

antipasti, Italian, 94

apricot and lavender mousses, 172

aubergines: aubergine, feta and broad bean salad, 96

  skewered lamb and aubergine pittas, 113

b

bacon: English breakfast salad, 21

  fusilli with Savoy cabbage and bacon, 57

bagels: mozzarella and tomato bagel melt, 21

baked beans: cheesy bean hash, 61

bananas: banana, apricot and orange blitz, 16

  chocolate banana cups, 175

  cinnamon pancakes, 19

bean sprouts: Vietnamese beef noodles, 51

beans: Boston baked pork and beans, 139

  butter bean and mozzarella burgers, 141

  cheesy bean hash, 61

  chorizo and cannellini bean soup, 59

  crusty Tex-Mex roll, 113

  stir-fried steak chilli, 54

beef: boiled beef and carrots with herb dumplings, 165

  dill pickle cheese burgers, 52

  stir-fried steak chilli, 54

  Thai beef salad, 134

  thick-crust beef and stout pie, 89

  Vietnamese beef noodles, 51

Bellini jellies, 170

best ever vanilla cheesecake, 183

biriyani, spiced chick pea, 61

biscuits: gorgeous cranberry cookies, 117

black eyed beans: Boston baked pork and beans, 139

blueberry pancakes, 175

Boston baked pork and beans, 139

bread, 20–1

  cheese toasties, 63

  crusty Tex-Mex roll, 113

  hot lamb baguette with mint and lime, 131

  Parma ham and mozzarella focaccia, 106

  vanilla eggy bread, 20

broad bean, aubergine and feta salad, 96

broccoli: long stem broccoli with chilli and lemon, 159

bruschetta, panettone, 173

burgers: butter bean and mozzarella, 141

  dill pickle cheese, 52

butter bean and mozzarella burgers, 141

butternut squash: butternut squash and Parmesan muffins, 116

  butternut chowder with cheese toasts, 63

c

cabbage: fusilli with Savoy cabbage and crispy bacon, 57

cakes: caramel ripple brownies, 118

  moist mango and maple cake, 123

  soggy belly chocolate fudge cake, 180

cannellini beans: chorizo and cannellini bean soup, 59

  stir-fried steak chilli, 54

caramel ripple brownies, 118

caramelised pepper spaghetti, 68

carrots: boiled beef and carrots with herb dumplings, 165

  roasted carrots with garlic, 158

chapatti, spicy omelette, 112

cheese: aubergine, feta and broad bean salad, 96

  butter bean and mozzarella burgers, 141

  butternut squash and Parmesan muffins, 116

  cheese and onion baked potatoes, 101

  cheese and tomato macaroni, 64

  cheese toasties, 63

  cheesy bean hash, 61

  crusty-topped shepherds pie, 163

  dill pickle cheese burgers, 52

  ham and cheese puffs, 29

  mozzarella and tomato bagel melt, 21

  pan-fried haloumi with fennel salad, 95

  Parma ham and mozzarella focaccia, 106

  Parmesan baked eggs and mushrooms, 22

  pea, mascarpone and mint risotto, 69

  potato pasties, 115

  quattro stagioni baking tray tart, 150

  red pepper and fontina cous cous cake, 100

  ricotta and basil frittata, 140

  roast salmon and goat's cheese salad, 145

  roasted pepper pizzettes, 67

  spiced chicken with herb cous cous, 42

  Taleggio and thyme risotto, 99

cheesecake, best ever vanilla, 183

chick pea biriyani, spiced, 61

chicken: chicken palm pies, 110

  chicken tikka wraps, 113

  chicken vindaloo, 44

  chunky chicken and potato pie, 80

  lemon chicken with sweet potato and rosemary mash, 81

  minted chicken and new potato salad, 157

  Moroccan chicken and pastina bake, 153

  oriental roast chicken, 156

  quick coq au vin, 139

  sesame chicken noodle salad, 111

  silky chicken noodle soup, 77

  spiced chicken with herb cous cous, 42

  sticky lemon chicken wings, 105

chillies: chilled fire soup shots, 95

  sausage piece penne, 58

  stir-fried steak chilli, 54

chocolate: caramel ripple brownies, 118

  chocolate banana cups, 175

  melting chocolate risotto, 179

  soggy belly chocolate fudge cake, 180

chorizo: and cannellini bean soup, 59

  chorizo omelette, 22

cinnamon pancakes, 19

clafoutis, strawberry, 178

clapshot, 159

coconut and jam tart, old-fashioned, 188

coconut milk: special fish curry, 38

cod: butter-roasted cod with spring onion mash, 34

coffee cream trifle, 172

coq au vin, quick, 139

corn: Vietnamese beef noodles, 51

courgette and mint soup, 139

cous cous: red pepper and fontina cous cous cake, 100

  spiced chicken with herb cous cous, 42

cranberry cookies, 117

crumble, oaty ginger pear, 189

cucumber: barbecued lamb leg steaks with summer salad, 49

  raita, 86

  spiced lamb koftas with tzatziki, 48

curries: chicken vindaloo, 44

  meatball curry with coriander breads and raita, 86

  prawn dupiaza with saffron rice, 151

  special fish curry, 38

custard tarts, lemon, 121

d

dill pickle cheese burgers, 52

drinks, 16

duck: Peking duck noodles, 79

dumplings, 165

e

eggs: chorizo omelette, 22

  Italian fried eggs, 24

  kipper and boiled egg hash, 28

  Parmesan baked eggs and mushrooms, 22

  ricotta and basil frittata, 140

  spicy omelette chapatti, 112

  vanilla eggy bread, 20

English breakfast salad, 21

entertaining, 94–5

f

fennel salad, pan-fried haloumi with, 95
fish cakes, haddock and coriander, 39
fish curry, special, 38
focaccia, Parma ham and mozzarella, 106
frittata, ricotta and basil, 140
fruit: frozen berry yogurt and meringue
    pots, 169
    panettone bruschetta with summer fruit
    compote, 173
    see also individual types of fruit
fusilli with Savoy cabbage and bacon, 57

g

garlic mushroom linguine, 68
goat's cheese: roast salmon and goat's
    cheese salad, 145
granita, lemonade, 169
Greek-style baked lamb with potatoes, 138
green bean, sesame and radish salad, 159

h

haddock: haddock and coriander fish cakes,
    39
    see also smoked haddock
ham: boiled ham in fragrant broth with
    sticky rice, 90
    ham and cheese puffs, 29
    see also Parma ham

i

ingredients, 8–10
Italian antipasti, 94
Italian fried eggs, 24

j

jam: old-fashioned coconut and jam tart,
    188
jellies, Bellini, 170

k

kipper and boiled egg hash, 28

l

lamb: barbecued lamb leg steaks with
    summer salad, 49
    crusty-topped shepherds pie, 163
    Greek-style baked lamb with potatoes,
    138
    lamb and red cabbage hotpot, 84
    lamb and red onion pilaff, 45
    lamb baguette with mint and lime, 131
    meatball curry with coriander breads and
    raita, 86
    roast shoulder of lamb with sticky
    pancetta potatoes, 164
    skewered lamb and aubergine pittas, 113
    slow-roast leg of lamb in wine, 85
    spiced lamb koftas with tzatziki, 48
lassi, mango, 16
lemon: lemon chicken with sweet potato
    and rosemary mash, 81
    lemon custard tarts, 121
    lemonade granita, 169
lentils: lemony lentil and pasta soup, 60
    sausage and lentil casserole, 137
linguine: garlic mushroom linguine, 68
    olive oil-poached salmon with linguine
    and lemon, 76

m

macaroni, cheese and tomato, 64
mackerel: quick grilled mackerel with lemon
    mint drizzle, 41
mangoes: mango lassi, 16
    moist mango and maple cake, 123
meat: Italian antipasti, 94
    see also individual types of meat
meatball curry with coriander breads and
    raita, 86
meringue: frozen berry yogurt and meringue
    pots, 169
Moroccan chicken and pastina bake, 153
mousses, little apricot and lavender, 172
muesli yogurt, potted fruity, 15
muffins, butternut squash and Parmesan,
    116
mushrooms: garlic mushroom linguine, 68
    Parmesan baked eggs and mushrooms,
    22
    quattro stagioni baking tray tart, 150
mussels, spaghetti with, 33

n

noodles: Peking duck noodles, 79
    satay noodles, 61
    sesame chicken noodle salad, 111
    silky chicken noodle soup, 77
    stir-fried pork and ginger noodles, 135
    Vietnamese beef noodles, 51

o

oats: oaty ginger pear crumble, 189
    raspberry granola, 15
olives: quattro stagioni baking tray tart, 150
omelettes: chorizo omelette, 22
    spicy omelette chapatti, 112
onions: lamb and red onion pilaf, 45
    prawn dupiaza with saffron rice, 151
orange, banana and apricot blitz, 16
oriental roast chicken, 156

p

pak choi: silky chicken noodle soup, 77
    Vietnamese beef noodles, 51
pancakes: blueberry, 175
    cinnamon, 19
pancetta: chicken palm pies, 110
    pancetta potato cakes, 23
    roast shoulder of lamb with sticky
    pancetta potatoes, 164
panettone bruschetta with summer fruit
    compote, 173
Parma ham: Parma ham and mozzarella
    focaccia, 106
    quattro stagioni baking tray tart, 150
pasta: caramelised pepper spaghetti, 68
    cheese and tomato macaroni, 64
    fusilli with Savoy cabbage and crispy
    bacon, 57
    garlic mushroom linguine, 68
    lemony lentil and pasta soup, 60
    Moroccan chicken and pastina bake, 153
    olive oil-poached salmon with linguine
    and lemon, 76
    sausage piece penne, 58
    spaghetti with mussels, 33
    tiger prawn tagliatelle, 127
pâté, salmon, 95
pea, mascarpone and mint risotto, 69
peaches: Bellini jellies, 170
    snowy saffron peaches, 184
pear crumble, oaty ginger, 189
pecan nuts: mango and maple cake, 123
Peking duck noodles, 79
penne, sausage piece, 58
pepperoni: quattro stagioni baking tray tart,
    150
peppers: caramelised pepper spaghetti, 68
    red pepper and fontina cous cous cake, 100
    roasted pepper pizzettes, 67
pies: chicken palm pies, 110
    chunky chicken and potato pie, 80
    potato pasties, 115
    thick-crust beef and stout pie, 89
pilaf, lamb and red onion, 45
pineapple: potted fruity muesli yogurt, 15
    stir-fried toffee pineapple, 175
pittas, skewered lamb and aubergine, 113
pizzettes, roasted pepper, 67
pork: Boston baked pork and beans, 139
    pan-fried pork chops with rosemary and
    spinach, 55
    salt and pepper spare ribs, 93
    stir-fried pork and ginger noodles, 135
    succulent pork roast, 160
potatoes: butter-roasted cod with spring
    onion mash, 34
    cheese and onion baked potatoes, 101
    cheesy bean hash, 61
    chorizo and cannellini bean soup, 59
    chunky chicken and potato pie, 80

clapshot, 159
smoked haddock and prawn pie, 74
crusty-topped shepherds pie, 163
Greek-style baked lamb with potatoes, 138
haddock and coriander fish cakes, 39
kipper and boiled egg hash, 28
lamb and red cabbage hotpot, 84
minted chicken and new potato salad, 157
pancetta potato cakes, 23
potato pasties, 115
potato stuffed poussins, 130
roast shoulder of lamb with sticky pancetta potatoes, 164
poussins, potato stuffed, 130
prawns: dupiaza with saffron rice, 151
smoked haddock and prawn pie, 74
Spanish prawn soup, 73
tiger prawn tagliatelle, 127

q
quattro stagioni baking tray tart, 150

r
raita, 86
raspberries: raspberry granola, 15
raspberry slush, 174
rough raspberry and almond slice, 122
red cabbage and lamb hotpot, 84
rice: boiled ham in fragrant broth with sticky rice, 90
lamb and red onion pilaf, 45
melting chocolate risotto, 179
pea, mascarpone and mint risotto, 69
prawn dupiaza with saffron rice, 151
spiced chick pea biriyani, 61
Taleggio and thyme risotto, 99
ricotta and basil frittata, 140
risotto: melting chocolate, 179
pea, mascarpone and mint, 69
Taleggio and thyme, 99

s
salads: aubergine, feta and broad bean salad, 96
barbecued lamb leg steaks with summer salad, 49

English breakfast salad, 21
minted chicken and new potato salad, 157
pan-fried haloumi with fennel salad, 95
roast salmon and goat's cheese salad, 145
sesame chicken noodle salad, 111
sesame, green bean and radish salad, 159
Thai beef salad, 134
salmon: olive oil-poached salmon with linguine and lemon, 76
roast salmon and goat's cheese salad, 145
salmon pâté, 95
salsa, fiery tomato, 128
salt and pepper spare ribs, 93
satay noodles, 61
sausages: chorizo and cannellini bean soup, 59
chorizo omelette, 22
sausage and lentil casserole, 137
sausage, onion and mustard soda farls, 21
sausage piece penne, 58
sesame chicken noodle salad, 111
sesame, green bean and radish salad, 159
shepherds pie, crusty-topped, 163
smoked haddock: smoked haddock and prawn pie, 74
smoked salmon tart, 146
snowy saffron peaches, 184
soggy belly chocolate fudge cake, 180
soups: butternut chowder with cheese toasties, 63
chorizo and cannellini bean soup, 59
courgette and mint soup, 139
lemony lentil and pasta soup, 60
silky chicken noodle soup, 77
Spanish prawn soup, 73
spaghetti: caramelised pepper spaghetti, 68
spaghetti with mussels, 33
Spanish prawn soup, 73
spinach, pan-fried pork chops with rosemary and, 55
spring onion mash, butter-roasted cod with, 34
strawberries: strawberry booster, 16
strawberry clafoutis, 178
swede: clapshot, 159
sweet potato and rosemary mash, lemon chicken with, 81

t
tagliatelle, tiger prawn, 127
Taleggio and thyme risotto, 99
tarts: lemon custard tarts, 121
old-fashioned coconut and jam tart, 188
quattro stagioni baking tray tart, 150
rough raspberry and almond slice, 122
smoked salmon tart, 146
treacle tart, 187
tatties and neeps, 159
Tex-Mex roll, 113
Thai beef salad, 134
tiger prawn tagliatelle, 127
tomatoes: cheese and tomato macaroni, 64
chilled fire soup shots, 95
griddled tuna with fiery tomato salsa, 128
Moroccan chicken and pastina bake, 153
prawn dupiaza with saffron rice, 151
roasted pepper pizzettes, 67
sausage piece penne, 58
tortillas: chicken tikka wraps, 113
treacle tart, 187
trifle, coffee cream, 172
tuna: griddled tuna with fiery tomato salsa, 128
tzatziki, spiced lamb koftas with, 48

v
vegetable accompaniments, 158–9
Vietnamese beef noodles, 51

w
wine: Bellini jellies, 170
slow-roast leg of lamb in wine, 85
wraps, 112–13

y
yogurt: coffee cream trifle, 172
frozen berry yogurt and meringue pots, 169
mango lassi, 16
potted fruity muesli yogurt, 15
raita, 86
spiced lamb koftas with tzatziki, 48

Acknowledgements
First, thanks to all my family and friends for tasting each and every one of the dishes in this book. Special thanks to everyone involved in the production of the book, to Anna-Lisa for her careful testing, great suggestions and help with preparing the food for photography; Gus, Vanessa and Will for making the book look so beautiful; and Janet for putting the whole thing together. I am especially grateful to Jane and Alison at Quadrille for their confidence in me. And last but not least, thanks to my favourite girls at Fork, my agents Sarah and Jerry, and my champion-taster – the handsome Roberto.